An Atheists
Unofficial
Guide to
AA

— for Newcomers

Copyright © 2011, 2013 revised, Vince Hawkins
ISBN–13: 1466209305

Not approved literature of
Alcoholics Anonymous

CONTENTS

Addressed to alcoholics

Chapter one – About this Book

This work is aimed at alcoholics put off Alcoholics Anonymous by the god content included in its literature and paraphernalia at its meetings like the banners on the wall showing the AA Twelve Steps.

It is not an alternative to AA but a demonstration that the AA program can work for anyone with just a few tweaks which flesh out the breadth of interpretations that can be put on it. There are as many ways of dealing with the program as people doing it. So this is an atheist version of the program. The object is purely to widen the net which catches the imagination of people who have been attracted into AA's ambit so that a greater number can get the program, giving up alcohol happily and becoming contented, decently functioning human beings.

I am mindful that AA freethinkers groups have started down this path with their own Agnostic 12 Steps. Half are changed from the AA original Twelve Steps. (Googling agnostic AA NYC or atheists AA meetings will produce information on non-religious groups.)

My atheist 12 steps provide alternatives for the same six steps, with two of these adapted from the Agnostic 12 Steps. This was after I reviewed the Agnostic 12 Steps to see if I could cut down any potential confusion due to too many versions of steps in circulation. It is important not to create confusion here, but to give choices to alcoholics who otherwise might not be helped. I feel this book completes a spectrum of views and beliefs against which to put AA in context: god-based – agnostic – atheist. For agnostics it now provides the other end of the spectrum from *Alcoholics Anonymous*, otherwise known as the AA Big Book, to consider where one sits. For atheists it should provide the assurance that the AA program can work for you equally as well as for a god-based AA member or for an agnostic.

Indeed I'd argue that my atheist 12 steps could be used universally by all alcoholics, god-based, agnostic and atheist alike. Moreover by substituting their prime problem for alcoholism, people – especially atheists, but anyone else – with other addictions and issues could be helped.

Steps 1, 4, 8, 9, 10 and 12 remain the same as the original AA Twelve Steps. These can be found at the beginning of Chapter 5 *How it Works* in the Big Book.

On the structure of *An Atheists Unofficial Guide to AA*, first this book helps a newcomer to address the essential question: am I an alcoholic? For those deciding in the affirmative or continuing to ponder the question we move on to the basic premise of accepting the need for change and stopping drinking as in step 1. Then we have to deal with the withdrawals, a process which can take up to two years like dealing with any post traumatic stress disorder. The timetable is adaptable just like everything else in AA, though it seems advisable to stick to the order of the steps as laid down. I worked on steps 1–3 over and over again in the early days while I went through the worst of the withdrawals.

Then this book suggests that, when ready, a member should get a sponsor or sponsors and embark on the remedial action contained in steps 4–9 to clear away the wreckage of the past. Later come the maintenance steps with daily self-improvement in steps 10–11 and, finally, helping others in step 12.

Next this book explains why this different approach from traditional AA is needed by atheists – and the importance of staying under the overall umbrella of AA. Then it addresses people outside AA: the family of a recovering alcoholic and the connections of an alcoholic who still drinks – family and employer. The A–Z explains terms used in AA that a newcomer or the connections of an alcoholic may hear without at first understanding what they mean. Appendix One deals with permission and non-permission from AA World Services Inc to reprint AA texts in this book; Appendix Two makes a further reading suggestion, Richard Dawkins' *God Delusion* – Chapter 4: Why there is almost certainly no God; and Appendix Three invites readers' ideas for entries in a future publication, *Atheists Daily Reflections.*

Sections of the Big Book to which I refer readers directly are Chapters 3 *more about alcoholism* and 10 *to employers*, parts of Chapter 2 *there is a solution* and Chapter 5 (above), and the Doctor's Opinion which is a foreword. Readers wishing to check out AA co-founder, Bill W's story will find that it forms Chapter 1 of the Big Book. Dr Bob's story (AA's other co-founder) and those of other early members are in the back of the Big Book.

I do not refer atheists or agnostics to Chapter 4 of the Big Book, *we agnostics,* but suggest readers who hold a religious belief refer to it. Ultimately this chapter does not accept agnostic views, let alone atheist ones: it implies that eventually, if one works the program properly, one is bound to share the god-based views of the majority of AA's founding members. I reject this idea unequivocally.

Chapter two – Am I an Alcoholic?

For the inquisitive drinker asking the question 'Am I an alcoholic?' the short answer may be obtained by answering this question: Do you have trouble stopping drinking once you have started? If so, you are most likely an alcoholic.

If still unsure, you may be able to define yourself as one of four types of problem drinker. These are based on the stages of addiction described in the Big Book for the benefit of the wives of early AA members. This will do as well for anyone – including drinkers themselves – grappling with the question of what sort of drinker a person is.

One – heavy drinker

Many people I secretly think are an alcoholic claim to be a heavy drinker. Since it is a self-diagnosis it is not for me to brand them as anything. Publicly I accept that what they call themselves is what they are. I may question their self-diagnosis in an attempt to get them to think about it more seriously, but I have to accept their answer.

The difficulty is that many people really are heavy drinkers who will change their behavior before, or as soon as, it becomes a problem – as soon as they become an embarrassment to their family or at work. They might claim their drinking does no one any harm, but heavy drinking will still slow you up mentally and physically, even if you don't notice.

Two – alcoholic out of control

Looking back, with the benefit of hindsight and schooling in what to look for, I can see when a large group of alcoholics graduate – when they can be identified and should be given a certificate. Many young people overindulge in drink but they stop at the family forming stage when the expense of a mortgage kicks in. This is when many an alcoholic stands out. Some get married, some don't but, when all their peers stop going out as much and lower their consumption, alcoholics just sail on drinking more and more. How can they afford it? They cannot. They overborrow on credit cards, steal from their life partners, steal from supermarkets or cut down on all other expenditure and start leading the miserable existence of an addict.

Many who admit to being a heavy drinker are really an alcoholic in denial: you completely lose control when drinking. Your friends think your behavior is over the top and no longer funny. You admit this, and protest that it won't happen again. Work may be affected. You may drink in the morning and/or through the day. You are sorry after serious drinking bouts and tell your partner you want to stop. But you can't stay on the wagon. When you get over a spree, you think you can drink moderately next time. If you display some of this behavior you are in danger. These are the signs of a real alcoholic.

Three – raging alcoholic, but you can be hopeful

I was somewhere between numbers two and three when I finally went to see my doctor and the chain of events started which culminated in finding AA. I can remember sitting on bar stools thinking I was free, that I could go anywhere. I always liked travel. But I might as well have been chained to the bar stool. I wasn't going anywhere. Near the end I wanted to stop drinking, but couldn't. (Now I have stopped drinking for 12 years I have real freedom to travel and am fulfilling my dreams instead of filling my head full of illusion and killing my body by degrees.)

If you are a raging alcoholic, you were once like number two, but you have gone much further. Now your friends have deserted you, you can't keep a job and your home is a tip. The round of clinics and treatment centers (they used to be called asylums) has begun. Either you pathetically hang on to the idea you'll one day drink like a gentleman or you badly want to stop. The chances of AA working in your case are good.

Four – far gone, yet you could get well

Maybe you are despondent after detoxing many times. You might be a violent or insane drunk. But no situation is hopeless. I know someone who had 27 detoxes and frequently drank on the way home from the clinic. He came to AA but couldn't get the message, in spite of suffering delirium tremens, until this 27th time of asking. If he could get it so can you. Another member was a former gangland enforcer who ended up living in the local park for five years – losing a kidney in the process. The surgeon told him if he drank again he would die. He even followed him out of the hospital into the bar across the road. Desperate, my friend – a member of my home group in the UK – asked another fellow member to be his sponsor. "On one condition," said the sponsor: "that you will be honest with me." Our friend was outraged at the suggestion that he might not be honest, but buckled down to the task and has now been sober for some years.

Longer answer

If still unsure whether you are an alcoholic, an even longer answer may be gleaned from the Big Book's Chapter 3: *More about alcoholism*. This is quite an atheist-friendly Chapter which I have no hesitation in recommending to readers.

I would only add a short note about the end of Chapter 3 in the Big Book: I assume that *divine* is not a word this doctor would have chosen today, especially as he says he is not a religious man. I'm betting he would have been happy with *spiritual* which, for my money, means greater than the sum of the parts in the field of human interaction (deriving from the combined activity of people who have an affinity in a group). The prime example I would give of this is how AA's early members invented the program – out of trial and error, human observation and debate among clever, also desperate, men and women. A second example is the same effect generated by AA meetings all down the years.

Chapter three
Step 1 – Yes, I am an alcoholic – Process of Change

Once you have decided you're an alcoholic, once the denial is over, how should you begin in the program? The way I started in AA was to read steps 1–3 and associated writings over and over again until I had accepted them thoroughly. Because of the mental dullness that comes with withdrawals this took me at least six months. However it is not a race – take as long as you like.

AA's general advice on the steps to new members is to be honest with yourself, remember you're dealing with alcohol – puzzling, sly, strong and uncontrollable. We can't deal with it alone. But we have the program, our sponsors, the meetings, the literature, other members and the AA fellowship to guide us through. The 12 steps are "guides to progress," says the Big Book. "We are not saints ... we claim spiritual progress rather than spiritual perfection." My definition of spiritual in this instance, by the way, is a serious and sincere attitude (see p33 below).

These atheist version first three steps suggest that we were alcoholic and could not manage our own lives; that therefore we needed the help of AA; and that we should practice humility by letting go of self-will. For this third step you will need to judge how tiny you are in the scale of things by realizing there are much bigger things than yourself. (This is not the same as low self-worth which AA will help to raise.)

Step 1 – effectively stopping drinking – is the only one which needs to be achieved 100%. **We admitted we were powerless over alcohol – that our lives had become unmanageable.** That is, by accepting unreservedly that we were powerless over alcohol and our lives had become unmanageable, we knew we had to stop. This is the end of denial. There is no need for blind faith. Look around you in the meeting room and see what it has done for others. You will find your faith in the process from the evidence before you. There is no difference in this step from the AA original. Atheist, agnostic, god-fearing, anything, nothing – it is the same for everyone under the sun in AA.

This is the surrender to alcohol. Admit that alcohol has beaten you and throw in the towel – this is the real victory. In this boxing analogy you don't get in the ring with Mike Tyson. That is how you beat alcohol – by not fighting it, not attempting to control it but giving it up. Anyone can prove they don't need AA by taking only a few drinks on each occasion – always stopping at or before a prescribed number, say three. Otherwise, try Step 1 once more. A word of warning about this business of trying to prove whether you're an alcoholic by attempting controlled drinking. Don't use it as an excuse for a relapse. I've known newcomers who grab on to this idea and you never see them again. If you have already been coming to a few meetings I'd count this as a relapse rather than the drinking-like-a-gentleman experiment. The experimental stage is right at the beginning. We know, really, that you're going to fail in this experiment but some prospects just have to find out for themselves. What's the point in confirming you're an alcoholic if you trigger many more years of drinking in the process?

I used the AA publication *Living Sober* for tips on how to navigate the withdrawals and recommend it to anyone else on the same journey. A good suggestion was to attend 90 meetings in 90 days. There is normally a choice of meetings so there is no need to revisit one you don't like.

I was told that the withdrawal process took up to two years like any post traumatic stress disorder following a stressful event such as divorce, a death in the family, moving house, changing jobs, or a new partner. Therefore, don't rush the program. The concentration required to abstain and get through the withdrawals, without a relapse, precludes starting on the self-improvement steps until later.

Also it is important not to embark on any of the life-redefining events just mentioned, if it can be avoided, in the first two years. The stress involved can break one's concentration on tackling the withdrawals.

I was also told that a relapse does not happen on impulse. If you are driving along on a sunny day and the thought comes into your head about how nice a cold lager would be, this simply sows a seed which grows until a week later you find yourself in a bar with a drink to your lips. Therefore, argue with such thoughts in your head. Tell them in no uncertain terms to go away. Don't let them become established. Drinking never can be an option.

'Play the film through to the end' was another helpful idea. If you're thinking how nice it would be to sit at a bar with a pretty girl sharing a bottle of champagne, go on past the initial picture to the gory details of what follows. How much would you really drink? How drunk would you get? What trouble would you get into? What harm would you do to others and yourself? Where would you end up? What pain would you cause to those close to you?

Stay out of bars unless you have a legitimate reason for being there. Put alcohol first. Don't worry in the initial stages about smoking. Smoke twice as much if you feel like it, eat twice as much chocolate. I was told not to worry about giving up smoking. It would happen when I was ready. And it did – 21 months later. It was easy, too, when I was successful in giving it up, compared to all the times I'd failed when it seemed difficult. Later I went to Overeaters Anonymous about the eating, but I recognized alcohol was my prime addiction.

If you absolutely have to attend an occasion, perhaps work-related, where there is drinking and/or you know you will feel uncomfortable, don't stay any longer than you have to. Always plan your own escape route in case. Make sure you have the phone number of a taxi or a friend if needed. In a pub situation, my first sponsor advised me always to buy the first round and slip away as soon as I liked. Usually no one remembers when we left, just that we bought a round, and if anyone makes a fuss about our not drinking alcohol it is a sign that they could have our disease, too.

The question of how to fill the time you used to spend drinking will arise. The cinema, evening classes, the gym and swimming are just a few examples. You could make your own list of things you'd intended to do. Also, you could sample many activities to see which ones spark an interest. If you are shy, amateur dramatics is a possibility, for example.

Process of Change

Change is an important concept for any alcoholic and the AA program is a process, not an event. I believe everyone who embraces the program changes over time into a happy, contented individual. This is the difference between adopting a program and white-knuckling it where one can stay off alcohol for a period but will remain a dry drunk – which is a miserable existence.

Believing it is possible to change one's attitudes is something that has happened to me in AA. I thought the leopard couldn't change its spots. I was a cynic, suspicious of people's motives and their actions, but now I am prepared to trust most people and don't think they're out to cheat me.

I have to be very careful now about branding people as a type before I assess them as an individual. Take the people some regard as the worst types. I still believe, for example, that politicians start off sincere and become corrupted. But now I would be prepared to believe that even a politician could revert to sincerity. I have met bankers, lawyers and tabloid journalists in AA who have definitely changed from the way they were. Most of them have retired so age could have had something to do with it as well as having made their pile, but AA makes better people of us.

One can even improve one's personality by minimizing the worse traits and building up the positive ones.

Another example is that I used to believe 'once a thief, always a thief'. But I have met plenty of former thieves in AA meetings including in prisons and followed up on progress after release – and it is definitely possible for a thief to change, too. I have changed my attitude to prisoners from 'they deserve punishment' to 'rehabilitation is the better option', cheaper for the taxpayer, too. There are bad, mad and sad cases in prison and most of them are sad. It seems that most committed the crime drunk or on drugs.

You can do it

Normal drinking means inhibitions lowered to remove stress, making for friendship, fun and relaxation – the good life.

But it was not for any of us AAs at the end of our alcoholic drinking. We wanted to stop but couldn't. Some of us sat at a bar wishing the words would come out: "I've finished" or: "a glass of water please," but all we said was "another" or "one more for the road." Some of us even thought we were free to do anything, but were really chained to a bar stool. Others were hiding away at home wishing to pour the bottle down the sink, but were necking it to empty the contents down their throats in the fastest way they could.

Old pleasures were distant memories. We fooled ourselves if we thought we could enjoy a social drink still. This time we thought we could control it, but we never did. My friend John said when he was getting dressed up to go out on a Saturday night he thought he'd meet a girl who would become the light of his life and everything would be happy ever after. He didn't think: "I'll end up fighting with the police and spend the night in a police cell again," but that's what happened. This was the insanity where we should have known from experience what would happen after we took the first drink, but we expected a different result.

Friends finally didn't want us around and we withdrew from life in the grip of an alcoholic haze. As we became lonelier some of us sank to sordid places in search of approval. Then we'd wake up not knowing what we'd done. Sometimes we didn't know where we were or who we were with. Alone, we would encounter confusion, fear, frustration, despair.

Some attempt suicide or just die from drink. In my younger years I knew I'd die early from drinking, but I thought it was worth it. I was lucky. When I was at my rock bottom a survival instinct kicked in and I changed my mind. At times alcoholics can stop drinking by white-knuckling it. But they won't have the contentment and reassurance of the AA program that makes stopping drinking a pleasure and a relief, once the withdrawals are out of the way.

I stopped drinking twice before I found the permanent solution of AA, the first time $22^1/_2$ years before, due to running into serious debt and needing to repair my financial situation. This lasted for a year. Then I gave my boss a lift to work because his car was being serviced and when I returned him home he invited me in for a sherry. Promotion beckoned, ambition kicked in and that was it for another 10 years of drinking.

The second time I stopped for similar reasons and 18 months later I was visiting a trade fair in Koln, alone in a hotel room in the evening when an electric light bulb pinged in my head: "I'll only drink abroad." That was another 10 years of drinking.

Many potential AA members say they are willing to stop drinking, but question whether AA is a workable alternative to the bottle. Some potential members worry whether they will become dull and miserable without a drink – this is how some define respectability.

It is not for everyone and there are other regimes available. One of the notices in AA rooms reads: "Try AA for 90 days and if you don't like it your misery will be refunded in full." Many rehab clinics and treatment centers, though, pass clients on to AA as a maintenance program thereafter.

My answer is yes, AA – or atheist AA if you will – is a workable alternative. It is a fellowship where you will find real freedom and friendship. Your mind will be wiped clean of the numbness and rust caused by alcohol. Life will take on meaning and you will become a contributor to humanity.

In all localities globally, alcoholics are dying helplessly like people caught in a tsunami. They cover the spectrum of social class and poverty or wealth. Among the survivors you will make lifelong friends, escaping disaster together, clearing away the wreckage of your past and then giving freely to help others survive and rediscover life.

If you feel these are overblown ideas for you and are saying to yourself: 'I couldn't do that,' remember you are no longer alone. With the backing of AA, what we individuals have accomplished "is only a matter of willingness, patience and labor," as Bill W put it.

Bill W was the author of the Big Book and a co-founder of AA with Dr Bob. The two of them met in 1936. Bill W had already had his last drink but was still having cravings, especially when feeling lonely, and was attempting to help other alcoholics as a way of diverting himself from drinking. He visited Dr Bob, having been given his name via a church minister as someone who was also struggling with drink and had not yet stopped. Dr Bob's last drink was on 10 June, 1936, the basis for AA's anniversary.

Bill foresaw a future which is well on the way to coming true. He dreamed that fellowships of AA would spring up in every hamlet. I hope that one day all alcoholics who travel will find an AA group including atheist AAs at their destination. (By 2010 there were over 115,000 AA groups in 150 countries with an estimated membership of over 2.1 million.) As it nearly says in the Big Book, join us as we stride purposefully along the road of happy destiny.

Process of Recovery

I am mindful to steer my readers back to the Big Book text wherever possible so that I am not the cause of any loss of revenue to AA. However this is not a matter of copyright in the US since all my references to the Big Book relate to the first and second editions where US copyright lapsed in 1967 – except for the additional material in the second edition where copyright lapsed in 1983. I have obtained AA's permission to publish outside the US.

In any event I have also tried deliberately not to pinch AA's big original ideas for this volume. Many of the fundamentals of the AA program were widely held long before it existed and some ideas were part of modern psychiatry when it was formed, so I am hardly stealing those. For example alcoholism is a disease which cannot be beaten by willpower; and, without help, alcoholics have no defense against the first drink. (After the first drink there is no stopping until trouble or oblivion intervenes.) These are the most important points made in the beginning of Chapter 2 of the Big Book. For the longer version of this beginning section I refer readers to the source, pages 17-24 of the Big Book.

This section ends with a description of the type of alcoholic targeted by AA. Simply, it is anyone with a desire to stop drinking. AA does not concern itself with interventions: if people close to alcoholics can convince them to contact AA, so much the better. But there is so much work to do among the willing that there is little point in knocking on doors and saying: "bring out your alcoholics." Some of us leave cards bearing the AA phone number with down-and-out drunks or crash victims, which can bear fruit. But as long as alcoholics are in denial and set against tackling their problem, we cannot help. We hope that when alcoholics reach their rock bottom they will have a moment of clarity and turn into a willing, or at least inquisitive, customer before it is too late. AA offers help to alcoholics who want to stop but cannot. Before AA existed, many were locked up. The alternative was permanent insanity or death. Nowadays we hope AA's existence will come to an alcoholic's mind at the appropriate time, maybe due to the seed planted by an AA school talk years before, or indirectly through information about AA we have delivered to doctors, magistrates, police and the like.

The rest of the second Chapter of the Big Book is about the process of recovery, aimed more towards the alcoholic, but connections of alcoholics may find the process interesting, too. It says that when we alcoholics first took a serious look at what the program would entail, none of us liked the ideas of self-searching, ego-leveling, noting of our defects and making amends to those we'd harmed. But we saw that it worked for others, and we had concluded that our drinking lives were hopeless and useless. There was nothing for it but to start assembling our simple AA toolkit.

Some members don't go through with the steps entirely. They are then left in a limbo land where they're better off than pure white-knucklers, but a great deal worse off than those of us who find contentment and pleasure in our new lives as a result of doing the steps more thoroughly.

The results include: the relief of identifying yourself as an alcoholic after years of denial; the pride of being honest with yourself and the beginning of building your self-esteem; managing your life better; replacing drinking buddies with new friends and activities; thinking through your ideas about gods and greater powers and choosing your own; knowing yourself better by defining your own personality traits and defects – minimizing the defects and accentuating the positives. You will clear away the wreckage of past misdeeds and make amends to people which is a great conscience-salver and another self-esteem builder; there will be the opportunity to deal with issues such as guilt over time when the balance of good deeds – including service in AA – will eventually counterbalance the bad ones. Service in AA, by the way, is a route to personal development, not just making sure the AA jobs get done. Then there is further self-improvement in the calming influence of meditation. Finally there is the task of helping other AAs and indeed people at large because the AA program is a bridge to normal living.

The Big Book also says: "it is no concern of ours what religious bodies our members identify themselves with as individuals. This should be an entirely personal affair which each one decides for himself ... Not all of us join religious bodies but most of us favor such relationships." The sentiment here seems laudable at first, but then I wonder if "ours," "our members" and "us" mainly amount to some sort of Christian brotherhood.

I'd rather it had said: those having religious affiliations or humanist ones or none will find nothing disturbing to their beliefs and ceremonies or non-beliefs. There is no friction among members over beliefs outside AA. It is of no concern if members identify themselves as individuals with religious bodies, non-religious bodies or none.

The part I agree with wholeheartedly, though, says: "This is entirely a personal affair which members decide for themselves in the light of past associations or present choice."

Chapter four – steps 2-3
Not alone and Letting go

We need a sponsor who will always be available for individual attention. Pick someone whose sobriety you admire and ask them to be your sponsor. You can have more than one sponsor if you wish. They fulfill the role of trusted friends. Nevertheless, you can fire sponsors whenever you like. They will help you through the steps and the rest of your life.

Here are the atheist steps **(in bold** where changed from the Twelve Steps of AA **and** *in italics where influenced by the Agnostic 12 steps*):

1) We admitted we were powerless over alcohol – that our lives had become unmanageable;
2) Came to believe **we couldn't solve the problem on our own, but that the group power of AA and the rest of this program** could restore us to sanity;
3) **We each nominated greater powers to remind us there are things bigger than ourselves, and not to play god – then we began to let go of self-will;**
4) Made a searching and fearless moral inventory of ourselves;
5) *Admitted without reservation to ourselves and another human being the exact nature of our wrongs;*

6) **Every few months made a shortlist of our defects most in need of attention;**
7) **Made it a project to minimize one or more of our worse faults and improve our behavior;**
8) Made a list of all persons we had harmed, and became willing to make amends to them all;
9) Made direct amends to such people wherever possible, except when to do so would injure them or others;
10) Continued to take personal inventory and when we were wrong promptly admitted it;
11) Sought through prayer and meditation to improve our *spiritual awareness and understanding of the AA way of life and to discover the power to carry out that way of life;*
12) Having had a spiritual awakening as the result of these steps, we tried to carry this message to alcoholics, and to practice these principles in all our affairs.

Not Alone

Step 2 – came to believe **we couldn't solve the problem on our own, but that the program and group power of AA** could restore us to sanity – requires us to accept that we cannot beat alcoholism on our own. White-knuckling it usually fails in time, but even if successful is a miserable way to beat alcohol. The AA program produces an individual who is happy, contented and a pleasure to be around for family and friends.

Why does this step need to be different for atheists from the AA original and from the Agnostic version?

First, the AA original. Actually this repairs an omission from the original Twelve Steps which skipped over the point about not being able to do it on our own. The original went straight on to introduce the idea of a greater power doing the work for you at this stage. This seems very dangerous and wrong-headed to me: the idea that you don't have to do any work yourself – let the greater power do it for you. The reverse is true. You need to put in a lot of effort yourself whether you believe in a duplicate god (power greater than ourselves), a god (call a god a god), or any crutch or comfort blanket to get you through – or not.

This earliest stage is when the withdrawals will be toughest. It gets easier as time goes on. But however hard you try, our experience has shown that you won't be able to do it on your own. This is why AA exists. If it wasn't there, we'd have to invent it. Oh, we did.

In a circular way the AA members who have been through this stage are now there to help you. Helping you does them good (it keeps them sober, is good for self-development and raises their self-esteem). So in the interests of transparent clarity, since newcomers' brains won't be as sharp as a pin until the alcoholic haze lifts off, it needs spelling out that you can't do it on your own and AA is there to help. AA is not mentioned in the original Twelve Steps, but it should have been to ram home the message that this is a place where you can get help.

There is also the small matter of powers greater than ourselves (other than AA) not being able to restore us to sanity as suggested in the AA Step. To mention a couple of examples of greater powers mentioned below in step 3: can a bus restore us to sanity? Can wandering around a field pondering "Isn't nature wonderful" restore us to sanity? No, we have to do that ourselves – with the help of AA members who have gone before.

A word of warning here. If you suffer from another insanity in addition to alcoholism, then we AAs are not experienced in dealing with other types of insanity and we advise engaging the help of a professionally trained psychiatrist for that. Preferably one who is sympathetic to AA helping with the alcoholic part of the problem. Some AA members have gone beyond their remit in the past and wandered into territory where they should not go. It has been known for members, when trying to help newcomers, to insist that they stop all prescribed medication. Areas beyond our knowledge and experience must be left to those qualified to deal with them. Newcomers must seek specific help for each part of their condition. AA, we suggest, for alcoholism and professional help in other areas.

Secondly, the Agnostic Step 2 substitutes "strengths beyond our awareness and resources" for "a power greater than ourselves" in the original. It also misses the chance to say we couldn't solve alcoholism on our own. But for the rest, I believe the different meat in the common sandwich "Came to believe … restore us to sanity" should specifically point to "the group power of AA and the rest of this program." I believe that in the case of this step experience has taught us that the AA program specifically, together with the group power of AA, is what we need. Both the original AA version and the Agnostic version are too nebulous and undefined to be of sufficient help.

Back to the plot:- Why can't we do the program on our own? Why can't we just buy the book and do the program in our spare time? Alcohol is such a powerful drug to an alcoholic, whose brain or genetic make-up or both combined are different from other people's, that it takes a whole battery of tools to beat it. Also each alcoholic's personality is different and they need a customized program which you can only get at the customized program shop – or the meetings of AA.

Regarding the insanity of our drinking: this is usually defined as doing the same thing over and over again (taking a drink) and expecting a different result, though any sane person would expect an outcome similar to those that went before. Look what John shares, related under *You Can Do It* in the previous chapter – that he imagined he'd meet a lovely girl and have a wonderful romantic evening when he went out every Saturday night. Yet he always ended up in a police cell. And there is a whole culture of insanity around drinking. Hiding bottles; buying drink at different places and believing no one notices we drink. I claimed to my first sponsor that I was an honest drunk. No one could have blackmailed me – it was all out in the open. Everyone knew which pub I was in. I was honest about it to my family – they always knew where to find me. "Really," said my sponsor, "and I suppose you told them how much of the family's money you were spending at the pub, too?"

"I wouldn't go that far," I said. That was my first pointer to rigorous honesty.

Now I've sobered up I can remember the look of horror on the secretary's face when I said: "if anything important happens phone me at the pub." And I didn't really always tell everyone where I'd be. I'd often sneak into a pub for a drink on the pretext that I was out on some errand. My nickname was Lord Shoelace because I'd pop out so often on a pretext like: "I'm just going out to buy a pair of shoelaces."

The way in which my whole life was a support structure to enable my drinking was a gross insanity I can see now. But I needed to be helped to see it by AA members, AA meetings and the AA literature. Skeptics may also wish to keep in contact with old friends and seek advice from family and other non-AAs to seek a second opinion as a checking mechanism.

How do we beat the alcoholic insanity? By staying off drink our minds clear and we start thinking logically and rationally once more. By talking to AA members we learn which traps we, personally, must avoid. By doing the program we reinforce our determination not to drink and how to be happy, contented and relaxed without it.

Meetings give direction on how to stop drinking, offer companionship and take up time – for time weighing on your hands can be a killer.

What to do

This is about the point in the Big Book where the Chapter 5 title "How it works" appears. I prefer "What to do." This is a much better title than "How it works" because the original Big Book Chapter 5 does not explain how the program works, but explains what to do.

Step 3: **We each nominated greater power**
there are things bigger than ourselves, and no
god – then we began to let go of self-will.

**Why does this step need to be different for atheists from
the AA original and from the agnostic version?** First the
original. An idea I have to discard is AA's *God as we
understand Him* expression to denote a greater power, or
substitute god. It leaves the member in the position of
playing Supergod inventing regular god. It leaves the door
wide open for imaginary greater powers which I see as just
comfort blankets that a grown up atheist AA doesn't need
any more. The only real function of the greater power once
you have stripped god out of the equation is to help
members right-size their over-inflated opinion of themselves
by comparing themselves to something very, very big. And
these greater powers should be tangible things that members
choose, not imaginary gods they invent.

Secondly, I prefer my step 3 for atheists over the
Agnostic version because mine offers more scope to adopt
any greater powers which could include the one proposed by
the Agnostics: "the collective wisdom and resources of those
who have searched before us." Of course this should also be
a tangible concept so it ought to mean living AA members
rather than dead ones. The living carry the wisdom of the
dead because it has been passed on by word of mouth. My
step 3 will not only allow the adoption of the Agnostic Step
3 if a member so wishes, but also any other greater power or
powers they care to adopt. In the case of rewriting this step it
was important to look for something new with plenty of

choice because of our experience that this aspect of the program has turned many people away from it. So this version of the step is designed to present new options and expand the membership, reaching out to those who would have been put off before.

Back to the plot:- Step 3 is the most spiritual for me. So I should explain what spiritual means to me at this point, even though the word is only mentioned in the steps at numbers 11 and 12. If you look it up in a thesaurus the synonyms are all religious – hardly fitting a non-religious program. But in dictionaries out of the four meanings given half are religious and half not. The first meaning I take in the AA context – or the Atheist AA context, if you will – is: *temperamentally or intellectually akin, connected by an affinity of the mind and/or temperament.*

Therefore a spiritual awakening or experience is an uplifting feeling on realizing one is part of a larger connected group in this way. It is a new sense of belonging. For alcoholics – who probably never particularly wanted to belong to anything – it may be seen how this feeling could take a while to permeate through, especially in the early stages when senses are numb from years of addiction.

The second meaning, already given in chapter two, follows on from the first: greater than the sum of the parts in the field of human interaction (deriving from the affinity one feels in a group.) For instance, as the prime example, this is how I see the process of arriving at the AA program in the Big Book – purely out of trial and error and human observation and debate among clever men and women. A second example is the same effect generated by each AA meeting all down the years.

Step 3 gives me an interim dividend from belonging to AA and a payback from treating the program seriously and sincerely, my third meaning of spiritual – in other words devotion to the program as it has saved my life.

This is what I mean when I say that Step 3 is the most spiritual for me. Not that it has any religious or other-worldly connection, but that it reminds me of how serious and sincere I am about the program and how devoted to it I have become. It also reminds me of my sense of belonging to the AA fellowship.

My fourth meaning is virtues for vices. Having thought long and hard (all I ask is that those who follow think it through and come to their own conclusions) I decided that my spiritual development should come from substituting virtues for vices in my everyday living: calmness and self-restraint for anger; tolerance for envy; balance for gluttony; generosity for greed; kindness and love for lust; courage for laziness; and humility for pride (this is the AA definition of humility which is a right-size view of yourself, nothing to do with being 'umble, and the AA definition of pride which is an over-inflated idea of your own importance, nothing to do with a job well done). That this format is like the St Francis prayer has not escaped me. Readers may like to write their own version.

Another non-religious meaning of spiritual given to me by other AA members is openness, being teachable, willingness to accept totally new views of the world.

The authors of the Big Book said alcoholism could be an illness which only a spiritual experience will conquer.

A great agnostic, Carl Jung, said something similar to an early member of AA, though his description was more dramatic and he seemed to be contemplating a more sudden change: "Here and there, once in a while, alcoholics have had what are called vital spiritual experiences. ... They appear to be in the nature of huge emotional displacements and rearrangements. Ideas, emotions, and attitudes which were once the guiding forces of the lives of these men are suddenly cast to one side, and a completely new set of conceptions and motives begin to dominate them." But as one of the appendices (II) to the Big Book explains, the AA conclusion is that spiritual experience need not be: "in the nature of sudden and spectacular upheavals. ... Most of our experiences are what the psychologist William James calls 'of the educational variety' because they develop slowly over a period of time."

This letting go can have the wonderful by-product of setting us on the road to finding ourselves. I have set out on a road to writing books and painting pictures. My hair is longer. I wear a suit and tie much less often, maybe two or three times a year. I am becoming happier day by day. My strong hope is that everyone on a Twelve Step program will set free their true self within as time goes by. I know of many members who have gone to university to facilitate a change to their favoured path. In this sense letting go can put us on the way to self-acceptance though this is more a focus of steps 4 & 5.

Let's not get ahead of ourselves, though. There are two aspects to this step 3. One is nominating our greater powers to remind us there are things bigger than ourselves and not to play god and the other is abandoning self-will, first accepting the theory and then applying it in our everyday lives.

Nominating greater powers

For members who have not yet chosen a greater power or powers, it is a prime job of your sponsor to help, but you must choose your own. Indeed, your sponsor will help you to define your own program, too. Both greater powers and program may change over time with your own development.

My own greater power is an amalgam of the literature, meetings and people in AA that have helped me to become sober and stay that way. It is a custom pick of the parts of the literature that make up my selected AA readings. I edit the meetings and people in the same way. I listen to everything they say. But there's a lot I don't agree with and discard in constructing my own program.

There is no reason why members should stop at nominating one higher power. The object for the purposes of step 3 is to realize how small we are as individuals, to help us gain a better idea of our self-importance when letting go of self-will. The only requirement then of the greater powers is that they are things you believe in that are big. Size is the issue here. Pick the biggest you can think of and then compare yourself with it.

Another common choice is nature. I am happy with this, too, as it makes me think of Darwin, natural selection and the power of the universe. Coincidence might be another one to remind us that most occurrences that some people put down to greater powers are coincidences. They happen a lot more often than many people think. Religious people will no doubt choose gods as their higher powers, but atheists need tangible greater powers.

Atheists need a tangible greater power

In addition to using AA or nature, other examples of tangible greater powers are the tree in a park in Dublin a former roofless drunk adopted (the one he used to sleep under and share his thoughts with); and the Number 9 bus because it goes past the pub that a fellow member could never pass until he got AA. My friend Michael feels his greater power − energy − through his emotions. This is tangible, too.

Albert Einstein once said he didn't believe in personal gods. I can see what he means. There would be so many of them, there would be chaos. And it makes the person the creator of the god instead of the other way round. As an atheist I feel the same about personal greater powers in AA. They turn the ordinary member into the role of supergod. Rather than an imaginary greater power, atheist members should pick a greater power they can see and touch − or feel − just to be sure it is there.

For any (most welcome) religious readers who have already defined their greater powers I suggest a reading of Chapter 4 in *Alcoholics Anonymous: We Agnostics*. It contains a surprising amount of material seemingly aimed at the religious believer. Just one plea before you go: please think it through. It is so heart-rending to see people sheep-like attending the services of organized religions. Do you really have your own greater power rather than simply subscribing to the political power base of a religious organization that might be doing damage in the world?

Bill W calls using AA as your greater power the simpler level. He takes a patronizing approach in the *We Agnostics* Chapter in saying: "it was comforting to learn that we could commence at a simpler level." As if a concept of a religious god was needed eventually. This I wholly dispute. In a similar vein it occurs to me that agnostics could try defining an imaginary greater power as a temporary measure until they can do without a comfort blanket and adopt a tangible alternative. But I do not wish to be facetious. I wish to be respectful and tolerant of every AA member's beliefs which are external to the fellowship. Bill wrote the *We Agnostics* Chapter at the behest of agnostics among the first 100 AA members, but the published message was not agnostic. What came out was: 'Don't worry if you don't get God at first – you'll get it eventually.' Bill says don't worry, that if you accept the principle that a power greater than yourself exists, then one day it will turn into God. And then he makes a schoolchild's attempt to convert unbelievers.

No doubt what the early agnostics wished to get across was that: 'AA isn't a religious program and plenty of atheists get it, too. If we get it, so can you – and there is no requirement to believe in any god at any time in the future, either.' My own creed is a belief in evolution through natural selection. Whenever I hear someone in a meeting starting on a creed – I believe in this or that god – I have an overpowering urge to share in turn: I believe in natural selection and I can show you chains of scientific evidence. Show me yours.

May I make one final observation. I think many people are too quick to attribute to God anything they don't understand. The catalogue of what we don't understand has been shrinking thanks to science, perhaps we could say for 2,000-3,000 years. I don't know anyone who now believes the world is square or that God created human beings through Adam and Eve in the Garden of Eden. We now know that natural selection and evolution account for this. Even bishops and for all I know the Pope himself no longer believe in the virgin birth of Christ. There seems no reason to me why this process shouldn't go on into the future until most things are explained by science and nothing is left to be attributed to God. But let me add that I keep an open mind on these issues and am tolerant of other people's beliefs. Just let me turn round one theme of the Big Book which is: 'don't worry if God is not your greater power at the moment – one day he will be'. My challenge to those who say this is: are you also open-minded? Are you willing to consider that one day you will abandon God and become an atheist like me?

A question may arise here. If AA is your greater power, why do you need step 2 *and* step 3? What is the difference between AA as mentioned in your step 2 and the allusion to it as a greater power in step 3.

For me the AA described in step 2 is a standard version for all members, whatever their greater power. The group power of AA in this step is the way in which all members work together to help each other.

If I take AA as a greater power in step 3 as well then this has a spiritual element. I am uplifted by the sense of belonging and I take the program extra seriously and sincerely in all I do. This uplift and extra seriousness and sincerity are equivalent to other members' religious greater powers. When I extend the principles of AA into the whole of my daily life I give it the central role whereas members with a different greater power may adopt a kind of power-sharing arrangement in regard to many matters.

Whereas I would call myself an atheist alcoholic, other members might call themselves an alcoholic Christian or a

Christian alcoholic. Either description may come first, similarly with other examples like an alcoholic Jew or a Muslim alcoholic. Alternatively you could just call yourself an alcoholic if there are no other affiliations whatever.

Abandoning self-will

We each choose different greater powers, so the secret of the common spiritual experience is in the letting go. For step 3 is about turning over or letting go. First we accept the big concept and then we apply it to our daily lives.

So the principle is that we alcoholics put ourselves neurotically at the centre of our world. We try to control people around us to achieve the outcome we desire. This is typically immature and simply asks for reprisals. We should be willing to accept that we are not the centre of the universe and able to accept whatever is inevitable. We need the willingness to accept inspiration and advice from others to practice letting go. Sane people let go. These should be our watchwords.

Balance should be the standard of our behavior and our greater powers may provide us with a mental compass. In addition to helping us right-size our own opinion of ourselves, helping us deflate our over-inflated egos, our greater powers can be the source of inspiration for a balanced life.

There are two caveats to this getting rid of self. The first is that we encourage newcomers to be selfish about themselves in the early stages when tackling the withdrawals. This is the part of their journey when they need to concentrate solely on themselves. Concern for others comes later.

The other is to be aware of the difference between selfishness and self-esteem. Many alcoholics have a curious combination of grandiosity and low self-worth. One of the jobs of the program is to build up that self-worth. It is a marvelous self-esteem engine which operates a hammer and a push-rod at the same time. The hammer is to knock down your ego and the push-rod – which moves vertically upwards – is there to build up self-esteem. This will conquer guilt and mean realizing that you are a decent human being. But, again, it's a process. This will come in due time.

The Big Book says: "the first requirement is that we be convinced that any life run on self-will can hardly be a success." Alcoholics are "an extreme example of self-will run riot," though they usually don't think so. Their troubles are basically of their own making due to their selfishness which, above everything, they must be rid of. On this basis alcoholics are "almost always in collision with something or somebody," even if their motives are good.

Now we must let go on a daily basis. I have been surprised at the effectiveness of this process of letting go. It has never let me down. I do the spadework on matters in my life, putting in as much preparation the best that I can. Then I let others come to their decisions that affect me – without bullying or manipulating anyone over the outcome. I just wait for the outcome to be arrived at. It is often a surprise, not the outcome I had expected, but it is always satisfactory and sometimes better than I had hoped. I believe this process works because I have fairer expectations nowadays instead of an overinflated view of what is fair and due to me – humility instead of an overinflated view of my own importance which, in the program, we would define as pride.

Of course I'm not a doormat either, but try to retain a right-size view of myself.

A by-product of abandoning self-will is not interfering in other people's lives and letting them make up their own minds about their own affairs. I don't take other people's inventory – in AA speak. The exception to this is when people sincerely ask me for my view. Sometimes I give it when I think it will only be taken into consideration and the person asking will make their own mind up. Sometimes I decline if there is a danger my approach will be copied slavishly without the person thinking the issue through. (However sponsorship, where a member asks for guidance, is a different case again where I feel duty-bound to outline as many options as I can think of and give an honest view of the direction I would take – but leave it to the sponsee to decide.)

The result of letting go and of the process working out satisfactorily is a sense that the program is magical, even if it is really only about managing expectations. Because I couldn't understand the process I even used to worry that a god might be involved, but now I believe the secret is in lowering my expectations: another key to the spiritual value of the steps for me.

The program seems to work in an interconnected way. Because I have learned the importance of humility, thinking of myself as less important has reduced the sense of what I deserve. Actually, deserve has nothing to do with it. Before I came into AA I was a very important person and deserved the best. I was so important that I thought people were talking about me when they weren't. Someone once said to me: "What makes you think you're so important that we were talking about you?" If only the idea expressed in

Rabbie Burns words could have helped me when I was drinking: "to see ourselves as others see us" … but I thought it was a marvelously clever idea that applied to other people. Now I must just wait to see what happens. My expectations are low and this is why I am usually happy with the outcome. Often it is not what I expected, but better.

Lowering my expectations is a part of my Step 3. A member suggested to me that it should be "no expectations" because expectations are resentments under construction and he had been told that attaining the goal of no expectations was part of the Buddhist concept of enlightenment.

To this I say we're not saints, we're just taking tentative steps on the path to sainthood which most of us will never reach the end of. Maybe we attain no expectations and then we die. Anyway, it's not perfection, but the working towards it that counts in the program. So I say lower your expectations. Keep lowering them. Maybe one day enlightenment/sainthood/whatever will be reached. I had another discussion with a friend about why Balinese people are happy when they are so poor. As an educated Balinese man, his explanation was that they have low expectations.

Taking Step 3 culminates in a prayer in *Alcoholics Anonymous:* "I offer myself to thee – to build with me and do with me as thou wilt. Relieve me of the bondage of self, that I may better do thy will. Take away my difficulties, that victory over them may bear witness to those I would help." However, the wording was optional.

This atheist author's Step 3 prayer is: "Please let me stick to my program." I repeat it as part of my morning routine whenever I remember and I have the distinct feeling that my days go much more smoothly when I remember than when I forget.

At this stage I should explain my attitude to prayer. I see it as a way of formulating thoughts and plans in my mind. It is purely a matter of keeping the motives in my mind in a healthy state. I don't believe it has influence outside one's own head unless one prays for someone and lets them know. But I experienced the power of prayer myself when I prayed for an enemy at the behest of my sponsor and it gave me a great release. I can't pretend that didn't happen just to placate the atheist right wing.

To whom are you addressing your prayers, then, an atheist has asked me defiantly. The answer is that the alcoholic part of my brain is communicating with the area which contains my AA program.

Chapter five – steps 4–9
Clearing the Wreckage of the Past

So far we have been mending our attitude which should have helped us to give up drinking if we were still not dry. Step 4 begins our action in the battle for sustained sobriety, a personal housecleaning which many of us had never tried. I believe it is probably best to wait until the drinking has stopped before tackling **step 4: Made a searching and fearless moral inventory of ourselves.** There is no difference in this step from the AA original. Atheist, agnostic, god-fearing, anything, nothing – it is the same for everyone under the sun in AA.

There are many ways of making a searching and fearless moral inventory. My suggestion would be to find your own best way. It may take a while to succeed, but is worth it. Examples are the Bill W method as in the Big Book and Dr Bob's method, also in the Big Book and described here in chapter seven. The first one I did was really a step 8 list written out in detail with the way I had harmed people. I did the second one together with a sponsee with whom I had followed Bill W's method initially. For our second attempts, for each of us, we sat down and considered all the bad character traits and all the virtues we could think of one by one. We scored ourselves on each one from one to five, depending how bad/good we considered we were and a pretty accurate list emerged with which to tackle the atheist steps 6 & 7 described below.

After a few years it will seem as though our personalities lean more towards the virtues than vices. We try to improve on the bad traits by shifting towards the virtues. Stating these bad traits and virtues in contrasting pairs produces the following list: selfish and self-seeking vs interest in others; dishonesty vs honesty; frightened vs courageous; inconsiderate vs considerate; pride vs humility; greed vs giving and sharing; lust vs what we can do for others; anger vs calm; envy vs gratitude; sloth vs taking action; gluttony vs moderation; impatience vs patience; intolerance vs tolerance; resentment vs forgiveness; hate vs love – concern for others; harmful acts vs good deeds; self-pity vs self-forgetfulness; self-justification vs seeing others' points of view; self-importance vs modesty; self-condemnation vs self-forgiveness; suspicion vs trust; doubt vs faith.

Here is the same list separated into its two halves: selfish and self-seeking, dishonest, frightened, inconsiderate, proud, greedy, lustful, angry, envious, slothful, gluttonous, impatient, intolerant, resentful, hateful, acting harmfully, self-pity, self-justification, self-importance, self-condemnation, suspicion and doubt; vs interest in others, honesty, courage, consideration, humility, giving and sharing, helping others, calmness, gratitude, taking useful action, moderation, patience, tolerance, forgiveness, love, – concern for others, good deeds, self-forgetfulness, seeing others' points of view, modesty, self-forgiveness, trust and having faith.

Another source of such lists is the specialist publishing house and operator of addiction centres, *Hazelden*. Another good method that could be worthwhile for alcoholics going through step 4 for the second time, say, would be to follow the *Overeaters Anonymous Fourth Step Inventory Guide*.

This is a Q&A book that can be filled in as you read through it and then shown to a sponsor.

To pick one of these possible methods to describe in more detail, The Bill W example of step 4 starts with our grudge list of resentments against everyone close to us but, beware, it is a beautifully laid trap, a con trick to lure us to the realization that it was our fault all along, thereby revealing our own character faults. You will need this list of people once more for step 8. There is no difference for atheists or agnostics in the wording of either of these steps from AA.

Carrying on from the step 3 theme of self-will, resentments – caused by personal relationships – are the most common sign of resultant problems and an alcoholic's spiritual sickness. But this method of step 4 teaches us how to draw their sting.

We write down our resentments listing people, institutions and ideas with which we are angry. So many emotions like anger and guilt mainly only hurt the person who harbors them, never the object of our displeasure. Against each name we write down the cause of the angry resentment. Big Book examples are: his attentions to my wife; she snubbed me; threatens to fire me for padding my expense account; misunderstands and nags. Then in a third column we write how this resentment affects us. Nothing counted but thoroughness and honesty, says the Big Book and, **in most cases, it was found that our self-esteem, ambitions, finances or personal relationships (including sex) were hurt or threatened.** After most of the points in the third column the example shows fear in parenthesis.

On scant perusal of our grudge list it seems it was other people's fault. But, if we only get this far, people usually continue to wrong us and we stay angry. The more we try to have our own way, the worse matters get. If we get a little further, and we blame ourselves, it is remorse. But this strong feeling of guilt and regret is no use either – it achieves nothing. So this list was just a starter to use as a guide to generate the real thing. Don't throw it away yet, though, you may be able to use it for step 8.

We must remove the other person from the equation and look at our own part in each issue of resentment. Referring to our list once more, blotting out the wrong others had done, we then looked for our own mistakes. Where had we been dishonest and selfish? When we saw our faults we wrote them down. This was the real first list of three. We might add other people we have wronged, but have no resentment against. This should include our entire close family. We admitted our wrongs and were willing to set matters straight.

Also, we reviewed our fears thoroughly. Thinking deeply about it, you will realize that anger stems from fear. Just when I thought I had mastered the impulsive jump from fear to anger after 11 years in AA it was demonstrated to me that I hadn't. I was navigating a zebra crossing in Saigon. These are completely disregarded by scooter riders, bikers and drivers alike so the only method is to take your life in your hands and cross. On the first occasion I found myself swearing at the traffic. Fear converted to anger in a milli-second. Somehow the traffic avoided me, though. And as I did it more often the fear and anger subsided. After 12 years in AA I had a similar experience in Chiang Mai, where you pressed a button, red lights were supposed to stop the traffic and you were given 15 seconds to get across. Even under these conditions drivers fail to stop and I was angry on the first occasion, shaking my fist, but I soon realized my energy would be better invested in spotting the cars that were not stopping and avoiding being run over.

Now we wrote down a second list under this Bill W step 4 method, this time of our fears, even though we had no resentment in connection with them. We asked ourselves if we had these fears because self-reliance failed us, if self-reliance didn't go far enough? Some of us once had great self-confidence, but it didn't fully solve the fear problem, or any other. When it made us cocky it was worse.

There is a better way now we are on a different basis; we let go of our fear to deal with calamity in a serene manner. Put another way, we will find the courage inside of us to face situations. When newcomers face difficult situations early on – and later – a good ploy is to say the serenity prayer over and over: "Grant me the serenity to accept the things I cannot change, the courage to change the things I can, and the wisdom to know the difference." Again, an atheist has asked me defiantly: to whom are you addressing your prayers? The answer is that the alcoholic part of my brain is communicating with the area where my AA program resides. I don't go in for acronyms as a rule but Face Everything And Recover is a good one alongside the alternative F*** Everything And Run – possibly run along Relapse Road.

Here is our third and final Step 4 list: we all have sex problems, it is a definition of a human being. We treat these as we would any other problem. We review our past conduct. Where had we been dishonest, inconsiderate or selfish? Who had we hurt? Did we unjustifiably arouse bitterness, jealousy or suspicion? Where were we at fault, what should we have done instead? We got all this down on paper and reviewed it. In this way we shaped an ideal for our future sex life. We must be willing to grow towards it. Under a future step we must be willing to make amends where we have done harm, provided that we do not bring about still more harm in so doing.

The Big Book concludes about sex by saying that if it is very troublesome, we throw ourselves the harder into helping others. "We think of their needs and work for them. This takes us out of ourselves. It quiets the imperious urge, when to yield would mean heartache." It continues on step 4: "if you have made an inventory of your grosser handicaps, you have made a good beginning. That being so you have swallowed and digested some big chunks of truth about yourself."

Perhaps, dear reader, at this point you can grasp an inkling of where the program is going. There should be self-improvement and in the future you should behave better. This, along with making amends and meditation, should make you a better person. Your good deeds including AA service will contribute over time to a reduction of guilt and the raising of self-esteem. Not every alcoholic has guilt, nor should they if past misdeeds were a result of drinking, an illness over which they had no control. But many do. My own experience was that the guilt-free illness line was one of the chief selling points of AA for me for a good six months. Then guilt kicked in and it took me eight years to get rid of it.

So there is a constant banging down of ego – for it grows back – and a raising of self-esteem going on in the program. This may seem an odd contrast, but think about how things were when you drank. Many alcoholics describe grandiosity (buying everyone in the bar a drink) going hand-in-hand with low self-esteem (feeling you're the lowest creature crawling on the earth the next morning). Step 3 is about getting rid of ego (a process for which you will later find additional support in step 11) and step 4 is the first stage in raising self-esteem, and there are more to come, particularly steps 9 and 12.

Step 5: Admitted without reservation to ourselves and another human being the exact nature of our wrongs. **Why does this step need to be different for atheists and agnostics from the AA original?** In broadly adopting the agnostic step 5 the major surgery involved is the removal of God from the AA original. For atheists there is no point in addressing God because there is no one there. The Agnostics have also inserted "without reservation" to remind us of the importance of not holding anything back. This is a point made separately, at length, in the Big Book. Members "had not been fearless and honest enough or shown sufficient humility until they told *all* their life story."

Back to the plot:- Writing down our defects in step 4 allows us to sit and peruse the script. This is the opportunity to admit to ourselves, the first part of step 5. Then we go to our sponsor or whoever has agreed to be our confessor and they check we have done a thorough job. We need this check because we are self-cheaters at least as much as cheaters of other people. Sharing with another human being means to borrow their brain, ears and mouth to check on the veracity of our "facts" and especially run an evaluation of these. We have admitted certain defects; we have ascertained in a rough way what the trouble is; we have put our finger on the weak items in our personal inventory, the obstacles in our path. Now these are about to be more roundly defined and tackled.

Most of us do it with our sponsor. Or we choose a sympathetic friend who can keep a confidence, ideally someone like our doctor or psychologist, suggests the Big Book. "It can be one of our own family," it says, "but we cannot disclose anything to our wives or our parents which will hurt them and make them unhappy. We have no right to save our own skin at another person's expense. Our stories' worst parts need to be told to someone who will understand, yet be unaffected. The rule is we must be hard on ourselves, but always considerate of others." Alcoholics belonging to a religious denomination which requires confession may go there, though they will sometimes encounter people who do not understand alcoholics.

The Big Book continues: "If there is no suitable person available, this step may be postponed, but only if we hold ourselves in complete readiness to go through with it at the first opportunity. We say this because we are very anxious that we talk to the right person. It is important that they fully understand and approve of what we are driving at; that they will not try to change our plan. But we must not use this as a mere excuse to postpone."

Usually we have a written inventory, though I have heard of cases where members felt it would be inadvisable, even dangerous, to write everything down. Anyway we are prepared for a long talk. We explain to our confessor what we are about to do and why we have to do it. They should realize that we are engaged on a life-and-death errand. Most people approached in this way will be glad to help. They will be honored by our confidence. We pocket our pride and go to it, illuminating every twist of character, every dark cranny of the past. "Once we have taken this step, withholding nothing," says the Big Book, " the feeling that the drink problem has disappeared will often come strongly. We begin to have a spiritual experience."

The person I chose for the confessional was my sponsor. He probed, prodded and tested some areas to help me to be completely honest and tell the whole truth. He thought many episodes I described were too trivial to be included, but I tried to leave nothing out. Having said that, though, the worst part was the way I treated my first wife and I did not relate the full brutality of my actions.

Some members make several honest efforts at a good 4th & 5th step and only reach a satisfactory point when they can say "that was it," after a while. In fact, it can never be done perfectly and new items will keep coming up, but the object to bear in mind is self-forgiveness and self-acceptance. In a similar vein it is often said that the step 8 list of people to whom amends are due must be headed by oneself. And the point of relating that at this point is to tie it up with the statement of one of my friends who said steps 4 & 5 were the best amends (under step 9) that he made to himself.

Virtually no AA member I have ever met believes that these defects are removed as is suggested in the original AA steps six and seven. More than that, I believe it takes continuous work on our part to minimize our defects and improve our behavior. This is why I suggest making it a series of projects over months at a time to reduce our faults – whichever one is worst, or few are worse, each time.

So the new **step 6** I suggest is that every few months we make a shortlist of our defects most in need of attention. This could be one worst defect or one or two worse ones.

And the new **step 7** is to make it a project to minimize the selected defects and improve our behavior.

Why do these steps need to be different for atheists from the AA original and from the agnostic version? My main argument for changing steps 6 & 7 applies equally to the AA original and the version of these steps for Agnostics. Both versions seem based on the implication that one's defects, or shortcomings, can be let go or eliminated. This simply doesn't happen in my experience and in the experience of all the people I have met and discussed this with, over more than 14 years in AA, bar a single person – whose testimony I don't accept. Therefore the object of my version of these steps for atheists – or anyone who cares to adopt them – is to identify and minimize one's character faults and keep minimizing them over time so that they become smaller and smaller and – just as one tries to achieve with one's ego – so they don't grow back.

Secondly, both of these original AA steps mention God. This makes them pointless for atheists. We do not know how many people throw up their hands at the mention of the word god and refuse the help that AA could have offered. This is just another example of religion doing harm. It is my fervent hope that more people will be helped by AA as a result of this book.

My third point here is spelt out at length, also as the third point, in chapter seven about religion being taken out of the original AA program, but then some being put back in at the point when Bill W wrote the Big Book Twelve Steps to replace the Six Steps which had been arrived at prior. I conclude that the original AA Steps Six and Seven were makeweights when the Twelve Steps were being written. Perhaps the author liked the sound of a round dozen. Perhaps because it fitted neatly with 12 months of the year.

Anyway they both mention god so I have replaced them with my friend Albert's suggestion which is self explanatory.

AA Step Six says: were entirely ready to have god remove all these defects of character. AA Step Seven says: Humbly asked Him to remove our shortcomings. But there is no Him. Once again, I have almost never met anyone who believes their defects will be removed. I have heard this step used as a hook on which to hang the importance of humility. But this is covered quite adequately outside the steps.

I suggested to a sponsee who believes in a Christian god that he discuss Steps Six and Seven with his priest. The priest's comment was that god makes babies perfect and that people become corrupted on their human journey. Well, I'm not sure I've ever encountered a baby in perfect shape and certainly they often have something wrong – from a hole in the heart to a hearing impairment in the case of my own children. Neither my sponsee nor I were any further forward after his talk with the priest. (Anyone under the misapprehension that babies have been made or designed by a single intellect, I'd refer them to Richard Dawkins' proof of evolution, *The Greatest Show on Earth*.)

Bill W's comment on extending the Six steps to Twelve was that breaking them up into smaller pieces would "better get the distant reader over the barrel" and "we might broaden and deepen the spiritual implication of our whole presentation." I cannot see how this applies to Steps Six and Seven. A more recent reaction from a member was that she uses these two AA Steps to perform a snapshot inventory of how she is behaving and minimizing her defects morning and afternoon or more often if necessary – but I believe that comes under Step 10.

Back to the plot:- Examples of defects that might be tackled under these new steps are anger and lying. Other lesser addictions a stepper has in addition to their prime problem could also be tackled here.

Anger takes me back to the feelings meetings in the clinic where I began my journey to sobriety. We were all addicts sitting in a circle and the course leader picked us out one-by-one and asked: "How are you feeling?"

We were all numb from years of using. One among us had just been talked out of his wardrobe after three days by his doctor. He was a cocaine dealer and user who had such paranoia. Another had been talked out of setting fire to the gas supply of his house, with a cigarette lighter, by the police. This had involved a full scale evacuation of his neighbourhood. And his was a sex addiction.

"So, what are feelings, then," I asked. A long chain of questions to the course leader and answers from her ended with: "So feelings are emotions, then?"

"Yes," she said, patiently. I was a journalist at that time, supposedly with a broad grasp of all subjects, and I didn't know what a feeling was. After weeks of entirely superficial feelings coming out along the lines of feeling up, feeling down, reporting on petty inter-personal bickering or contacts with family which would bring out something like "he or she really pisses me off," someone said: "I feel angry." Then someone else said: "I feel angry, I feel more angry than you." We had an anger competition. That opened the floodgates and the emotions came streaming out. Grown men were often in tears, let alone the women. The women apologized through their tears I remember – "I'm sorry, blub, blub, blub." But the men didn't. Suddenly it was an OK, manly thing to do.

Anger is the defect that has needed the most work in my case. Smart remarks is another, but that's another story. Lying is a further common example of a defect suitable for project work under step 7. We all do it, there are lines to be drawn where it is kinder not to tell the whole truth, but if we are dishonest in our dealings there will be repercussions from people we hurt. How are we to behave better unless we are honest? There is also the problem of not being honest with ourselves if we are not so with others. That will give us the handicap of an unreal perception of people, events and issues around us which will lead to bad decisions.

I used to draw the line in my work between people who "believed their own bullshit" and the rest of us. The former group were so dishonest as a habit that it had seeped into their personal perceptions. They were usually selling dubious products and services. I was around such people because I was on a downwards slide in my career due to drinking. Curiously, I was a successor of Bill W who had started out by visiting companies as a basis for advice on stocks and shares. I was an investment analyst. I had begun working for stockbrokers of good repute, but had ended writing notes on cheap companies, dressing them up as good investments when they were out-and-out gambles, for a sweatshop full of telephone lines and salesmen with plummy accents who defrauded unsuspecting clients. "I know the last one was a dud, but this one will get all your money back and more."

Everyone seemed to have alibis from "I'm just doing what I'm told" to "I've a family to feed and I can't just walk out until I have another job." I stole from my family in my drinking career in the sense that what I spent on drink should have been spent on them. I'm not always honest in recovery either. The most recent example was a taxi driver who I think may have been drunk because he gave me more in change than I gave him for the fare. While I was thinking: "he won't even notice in the morning, he shouldn't be driving drunk – it serves him right," he had driven off smartish. If my thinking had been a bit clearer and quicker I would have concluded that it was about me being honest sooner. But after I counted the money in my hand he had disappeared round a corner. Thinking now, I should have grabbed him and written down the local AA number for him or a message saying phone Alcoholics Anonymous.

My other addictions are mainly orange tarts with vanilla yogurt, a chocolate cake in a glass called a sexy cappuccino and a lemon coconut meringue. You get the picture. I have been to Overeaters Anonymous and given up sugar for a time, though I'm in relapse at the moment. In no way is this as serious as alcoholism on my scale of addictions. Alcohol is unquestionably the prime one and it is important always to put it first. However, overeating is a defect of mine that I can address under these new steps.

Under the original AA steps I found it difficult to combine the two programs when I went to OA (only with alcohol changed to food in Step One and "to alcoholics" deleted from Step Twelve). But I found it confusing because of the need for a different greater power. But the new atheist steps give me a much easier framework. Some greater powers can be common. And OA can be substituted for AA in the atheist steps 2 and 11.

Thanks are due to my friend Albert for suggesting these replacement steps 6 & 7. I was going to delete the old ones and reduce the number of steps for atheists to 10. But, rather like the early member who convinced Bill W to insert

Chapter 4 *to agnostics* into the Big Book and the words "as we understand him" after the mention of god in the twelve steps, I have been convinced that it is a better idea to insert replacements. Albert told me that his own version of steps 6 and 7 are his favorites of the 12 steps. I have heard Christians say the same thing about the old Steps Six and Seven. So now all members have the opportunity to choose a version which could be their firm favorites for many years. Work on these new atheist steps 6 and 7 can go on independently of continuing with the other steps – and taking a daily inventory as suggested in Step 10 – or in conjunction with them.

Now for the first time we need to make contact with people outside AA – though we know them – via **steps 8 and 9.**

8) Made a list of all persons we had harmed, and became willing to make amends to them all;
9) Made direct amends to such people wherever possible, except when to do so would injure them or others.

There is no difference in these steps from the AA originals. Atheist, agnostic, god-fearing, anything, nothing – it is the same for everyone under the sun in AA.

Step 8: we made a list of persons we have harmed and to whom we are willing to make amends when we did step 4 – all of those close to us and anyone else we have hurt badly. This could be reviewed with one's sponsor to check that too trivial matters are not included and that no one important has been overlooked. This usually means yourself. Sometimes a great deal more is made of willingness in general when taking this step. Actually I don't think willingness is the issue here. There is bound to be apprehension, but we must do it anyway. We must go to any lengths for victory over alcohol. Willingness in the abstract is like blind faith. I'd rather you showed me the evidence and let me make up my mind on a case by case basis.

Step 9: now we visit those we have harmed and try to repair the damage. Those who have moved a long way away we can phone or, if more appropriate, we can write – including to those who have since died. For slighter matters an apology will suffice, but for those close to us it will be a process that lasts to the end of lives.

Most of us owe money when we stop drinking and cannot meet all of our creditors' terms. We must explain that we are sorry our alcoholism has made us slow to pay, but that we have reformed and are trying to repair our fences. We must be honest and arrange the best deal we can, perhaps with the benefit of advice from a reputable charity like the Citizens' Advice Bureau in the UK. We must go to any length because if we are afraid to face our creditors we may drink. But we should not be predicting the outcome. The most ruthless creditor can surprise us with a pragmatic attitude.

How do we approach the person we hated, who has done more harm to us than we have to them? In no way do we express disapproval of such a person, nor tell them what they should do. We forgive them without saying anything about it. We mention our former illfeeling and express regret. We tell them we have given up our earlier drinking lifestyle and are on a mission to clear the wreckage of our past lives as part of a fresh start without drink. It does not matter if someone throws us out or won't see us. We have done our part.

Our guiding principle is to do the right thing, no matter what the personal consequences might be. Ultimately we must be willing to sacrifice a job, go to jail, or ruin our reputation if that is required by other people involved. However, AAs can often do more to repair the damage if they stay out of jail than if they go in. Therefore we should not play the foolish martyr who rushes in to save himself while leaving others worse off than need be. We should always secure consent to our plans from other parties involved.

It is likely that we have domestic issues. Perhaps the alcoholic has had an affair with someone who understands. If we are sure our partner does not know, should we tell them? Not always – it may be kinder not to.

Even without such difficulties, there will be lots to do at home. Sobriety is only the start. A mumbled apology will not be nearly enough. We ought to gather the family and honestly analyze the past, but without criticizing them. Their flaws may be obvious, but our own actions are probably partly to blame. So we begin our amends to the family. We must remember that 10 or 20 years of drunkenness will make a skeptic out of anyone, but it never ceases to amaze me how much suffering people will put up with in the first place and how forgiving they will be afterwards.

There may be some wrongs we can never fully right, says the Big Book. We don't worry about them if we can honestly say to ourselves that we would right them if we could. Some amends will need to continue for a lifetime. These will include improving behavior. There may be a valid reason for postponement in some cases. But we don't delay if it can be avoided.

Chapter six – Daily Maintenance – steps 10-12

Step 10 proposes a nightly personal inventory, setting right any new mistakes and regularly checking progress on step 7, but it is not an overnight matter. It should continue for a lifetime. (Continued to take personal inventory and when we were wrong promptly admitted it.) **There is no difference in this step from the AA original. Atheist, agnostic, god-fearing, anything, nothing – it is the same for everyone under the sun in AA.**

When dishonesty, fear, resentment or selfishness arise, if we have harmed anyone, we make amends quickly. We are not saints and still get angry and so on, but can be aware of it and keep improving slowly. Tolerance and care for others are our watchwords. So then we cast our minds about to someone we can help. This will be a natural reaction if you have already progressed to step 12. If you haven't yet begun on step 12 use this as an opportunity for a little pre-taster.

Here is another example of the flexibility of the program for me. I generally fall asleep as soon as my head touches the pillow and I don't like to interfere with this process by interposing bedtime routines.

But I'm an early riser – usually up with the sun – and so I do my step 10 in the morning along with my step 11 morning meditation.

By this stage of the program, says the Big Book, we have stopped fighting anything or anyone, especially alcohol. If tempted we will react sanely and normally – recoiling from it as from a hot flame – and we find that this has happened automatically without any thought or effort on our part. That is our experience. We are not fighting alcohol, neither are we avoiding temptation. We are neither cocky nor are we afraid. We have not even sworn off. Instead, the problem has been removed. It does not exist.

This is another aspect of the process for which I could once find no short rational explanation and therefore I found it magic and was worried that it might be god-induced. It still seems spiritual in the non-religious sense. But now I think it can in part be explained by the alcoholic haze in the brain clearing over time so that this rational aversion to alcohol is asserted. Attending AA and maintaining the program is a big part, too. But it is possible for this seemingly secure state of affairs to be undone. The Big Book warns that it is easy to let up on the program and rest on our laurels. We are headed for trouble if we do, for alcohol is a subtle foe. We are not cured of alcoholism. What we really have is a daily reprieve contingent on the daily maintenance of our program.

Step 11 suggests prayer and meditation. (Sought through prayer and meditation to improve our spiritual awareness and our understanding of the AA way of life and to discover the power to carry out that way of life.)

Why does this step need to be different for atheists from the agnostic version and from the AA original? First the difference from the agnostic version is much more slight than it may at first appear. I have left in the words "prayer and" from the AA original. My agnostic friend Albert has warned me that these words will be anathema to atheists. But I can only go on my own experience. First I must make it plain my definition of prayer has no religious or other-worldly connotation whatever. The dictionary definition I favour is "to hope strongly." And, as I say elsewhere in this book, I discovered the power of prayer myself when I prayed for an enemy at the behest of my sponsor and it gave me a great release. I don't believe it has influence outside one's own head unless one prays for someone and lets them know. Letting people know you are saying a prayer for them, even if you also tell them about your doubts that it does any good, can spread a little happiness a long way. I simply think of it as wishing people well – purely a matter of keeping the motives in one's mind in a healthy state. For me a prayer is just like wishing someone a safe journey. What harm can there be in spreading a little happiness and reassurance by letting someone know you wish them well?

Even if you keep it to yourself, it will act as a check that one's motives are proper, which can only be improving one's own state of mind. Nevertheless a spirititual life without prayer is clearly possible and the inclusion of prayer in this step is a matter of choice. The rest of this step is the same for atheists as for agnostics since I have adopted this part of the Agnostic version.

So, secondly, the difference from the AA original is to delete the *God as we understood Him* reference and replace it with improving our spiritual awareness and our understanding of the AA way of life and to discover the power to carry out that way of life. The reasons for this change from an atheist's perspective are the belief that there is no god; the need to stress that nevertheless spiritual awareness can be a rewarding non-religious experience; to explain the AA program as a way of life (some say a bridge to normal living); and to remind us that we will find the power in ourselves to change ourselves for the better.

Back to the plot:- On awakening I repeat my Step Three prayer; "please let me stick to my program." I consider my plans for the day. Sometimes I make a list of tasks but I never attach a deadline. I just put them in order of priority. As a journalist I once attended a Coroner's Inquest into the death of a company director who had jumped from the top of a car park. His widow gave evidence that he would make a list each morning and break down each night because he had only accomplished one or two tasks in that day.

Spiritual Awareness

Then I meditate for a short period and leave my mind free to wander where it will. Sometimes it wanders to a shopping list. I think this reflects a contented, unworried state of mind. Sometimes a step 10 issue comes to the forefront of my mind where I owe an apology, or a way in which I can help someone occurs to me. Other people prompt the subjects of their meditation by feeding themselves topics. Thinking of one's family, friends and acquaintances is a good idea and asking if we show kindliness, love, patience and tolerance.

While some use the Buddhist method of listening to their own breathing to calm themselves down for meditation, atheist AAs must do some research and find what will work for them. A practice like Transcendental Meditation can be helpful. I once heard a monk advise a person who was having trouble meditating to keep trying. "Any learning process is like learning to ride a pushbike," he said, "you will often fall off before you master it." A doctor taught me to hypnotise myself many years ago as a method of calming myself down after I went to him over anger issues. So this is my method of meditation. I used to stare at a penny taped to the wall, but do not need this part anymore. I used to imagine walking down warm steps from a balcony on to a sun-drenched beach and lie on a sunbed, relaxing each of my limbs and parts of my body from the tips of my toes to the top of my head in turn. I still use this method when attending my favourite Step Eleven meeting in Ubud. Doing it anywhere else I am immediately transported to that location at the back of the football ground on Monkey Forest Road and drift off in a moment. I can feel the warmth, hear the lovely sound of schoolchildren, see ant traffic moving both ways along a wire and feel beautifully relaxed.

For me, meditation helps in the process of substituting virtues for vices in an automatic way. For example, where there was anger it leaves me calmer, where there was ego there is nothingness, where there were resentments it leaves me tolerant, understanding and wishing to do good. It leaves me open, teachable and willing to accept totally new views of the world. If this is another point where religious believers see god taking a hand, all I see is a process by which one lets go of negative thoughts, thereby leaving room for positive ones to flourish. We move into a state where we observe our thoughts without giving them any power. But in letting go of the negative, all that is left when we emerge is the positive. Once again, we are after progress, not perfection.

Another aspect of this step is to extend the program into everything we do.

Bridge to Normal Living

We can be kinder to strangers, not just to our family and friends. We can apply AA principles to our work life, not just to interaction with AA members. The Big Book adds some useful suggestions at this point such as asking family and friends if they would like to join us in morning meditation. If we encounter stress as we go through the day we can repeat our own step 3 prayer or the Serenity prayer which seems to have been adopted by AA members and spread to others: "Grant me the serenity to accept the things I cannot change, the courage to change the things I can and the wisdom to know the difference." Thus, "we remind ourselves we are no longer running the show," letting go of self-will. "We are then in much less danger of excitement, fear, anger, worry, self-pity or foolish decisions. We become much more efficient. We do not tire as easily, for we are not burning up energy foolishly as we did when we were trying to arrange life to suit ourselves."

This point about applying the program outside AA is a part of the next step, too. We will not only carry the message to other alcoholics, but also apply these principles in all our affairs. This means doing a good turn for other members of the human race. The *Just for Today* card is another piece of AA literature that contains some good ideas – and it is free. For instance, it suggests that at least one good turn you do each day should be kept secret from your acquaintances. I'd love to list all of my good works here, but alas I can't or they will not count …

This feeble joke is not a license to refrain from sharing at meetings about your Step 12 work. I'm sure good AAs do more than one good deed a day – they are not limited by a boy scout code – and need only keep one such deed secret.

Power to Change for the Better

The more I practice the program the easier it becomes. There are moments of blind faith required when one first tries something new, but I learn these things have worked for others. Once I know from experience that they can work for me, I am less apprehensive about repeating them. It is not a question of whether behaving well "works." It is that behaving badly does not work. Where I have shouted, bullied and manipulated people in the past, I now know they will have got their own back in some way. Having tried the program's method of letting go and accepting unexpected outcomes, I now believe that when I got my own way in the past, I would usually have been better off if there had been a different outcome that I hadn't forced.

I believe the power to change for the better is implicit in the program and one is empowered by other people in the program. We get stronger spiritually and develop as people as we progress through the program. Doing AA service, for example, is not just a matter of getting the AA jobs done as I once suspected. It contributes to individual development and raises self-esteem with all sorts of spin-off benefits such as relieving guilt over time.

The Big Book also talks about pure motives helping in this process, which reminds me not to be irritated when a religious person says: "I prayed this morning that my god will look after all AA members so even if you don't believe in a god, my god is looking after you, too." Like so many things, my attitude to this depends on the motive. If the religious person is teasing, then it is not well meant, but it is best to assume he is sincere and wish him well in return – or that it is a harmless joke and enjoy it as such.

Step 12

Twelfth-stepping applies equally to newcomers and to help people to stay in the program and keep growing. Most AAs get down periods in the program and need support to continue.

These days (writing in 2011) AA telephone numbers and meetings are advertised around the world on the internet and in the press. New prospects may get in touch by telephone or turn up at a meeting as a result of family pressure, referral from a treatment center or a court, or because of their own desperation. Where there is a helpline telephone number, AA members in the role of telephone responders answer prospects' phone calls and arrange for another AA member, the twelfth-stepper, to make the initial personal contact. In these circumstances the main task is to make sure that the prospect attends their first few meetings. (We usually say: "please try at least six meetings and if you don't like one, try another.")

If this work is fully covered and an AA member who has progressed to the twelfth step has done what they can to help long term members, they may wish to be more proactive. In these circumstances – or if conditions are more basic in a developing country, say – then the rudiments of the old Big Book Chapter 7 on this step still apply. **Step 12**: Having had a spiritual awakening as the result of these steps, we tried to carry this message to alcoholics, and to practice these principles in all our affairs. **There is no difference in this step from the AA original. Atheist, agnostic, god-fearing, anything, nothing – it is the same for everyone under the sun in AA.**

Spiritual Awakening

The acquisition of a spiritual side will often start early on in our AA journey. In any event it will most likely have been acquired by the time a member reaches step 12, and it never seems to be static. A minority claim a big bang experience of a spiritual conversion. But I have always been dubious about all-singing, all-dancing white light experiences in hospital beds when a patient is pumped full of drugs.

No two seem to be the same: "maybe there are as many definitions of spiritual awakening as there are people who have had them," it is suggested on page 106 in one of the AA books, *The Twelve and Twelve.*

If one looks in a thesaurus, spiritual can mean holy, pious, religious, sacred and saintly. These do not fit with a non-religious program so I can only pick out devout as an appropriate synonym which can also mean serious and sincere. These last two words reflect my attitude to the program as it has developed after living by it for 12 years. So I interpret spiritual as serious and sincere. This does not preclude lots of other facets of a personality such as happy and fun-loving. In the context of step 12, I would add open and tolerant. There is also a sense of wanting to help and do the right thing.

There is a huge difference between our condition on first coming into AA and on reaching step 12. It shows us how far we have come. At first we were best advised to stay away from bars and temptation. But now, assuming we are spiritually fit, the Big Book says we can do all sorts of things alcoholics are not supposed to. "People have said we must not go where liquor is served; we must not have it in our homes; we must shun friends who drink; we must avoid films with drinking scenes; our friends must hide their bottles if we go to their houses; we mustn't think or be reminded about alcohol at all. Our experience shows that this is not necessarily so."

The advice is to let friends know they are not to change their habits on your account. The placement of this advice under step 12 is no coincidence. It gives plenty of time after entering the program to find out who your true friends are. At an appropriate time explain to friends why alcohol disagrees with you. If you do this thoroughly, few people will ask you to drink. If someone pesters you to drink it is a sign they might need the help of AA themselves. While you were drinking, you were isolating from life little by little. Now you are getting back into the social life of this world. Don't start to withdraw again just because your friends drink liquor.

My wife kindly offered to ask me if her having a drink would make me uncomfortable during the early stages, but I only ever said "yes" once and soon told her it was unnecessary. In fact any plan to deal with alcoholism which shields the sick person in the long run from temptation is doomed. It may succeed for a time, but usually leads to a bigger booze-up than ever. So the rule is: "not to avoid a place where there is drinking, *if we have a legitimate reason for being there.*" That includes bars, dances, nightclubs, parties, receptions and weddings.

Note the qualification. Ask yourself if you have a good business, personal or social reason for going on each occasion. Or are you expecting to steal a little vicarious pleasure instead? If you go to the place, be sure you are on solid spiritual ground before you start – that you are sticking to your program – and that your motive is thoroughly good.

Are you thinking what you can bring to the occasion rather than what you will get out of it. If you are shaky, it may be better not to attend.

"Your job now," says the Big Book, "is to be at the place where you may be of maximum helpfulness to others, so never hesitate to go anywhere if you can be helpful. You should not hesitate to visit the most sordid spot on earth on such an errand." Keep on the firing line of life with these motives and your practice of the 12 steps will keep you unharmed.

The first 100 AAs add a postscript in the Big Book: "we are careful never to show intolerance or hatred of drinking as an institution ... new alcoholics look for this spirit among us and are relieved when they find we are not witchburners. Some day we hope that Alcoholics Anonymous will help the public to a better realization of the gravity of the alcoholic problem, but we shall be of little use if our attitude is one of bitterness or hostility. Drinkers will not stand for it.

"After all, our problems were of our own making. Bottles were only a symbol. Besides, we have stopped fighting anybody or anything. We have to."

There is plenty of opportunity these days to reach out to the public and use public service channels as a way of informing everyone globally that AA exists – so that every alcoholic will find out that it offers an option if they want to stop drinking. Anyone representing an AA group in its wider district or region should be willing to introduce you to the right person for contacting schools, the police, magistrates, hospitals, doctors and the like with information on AA. Just remember that under the AA Traditions this is not meant to be a promotional exercise, simply to alert the public that AA exists to help people who want to stop drinking.

Service in AA doesn't just get essential tasks done. It helps in the self-development of individuals in the program, often playing a part in the right-sizing of egos through the cut and thrust of working with others, and raises their self-esteem. "If you want self-esteem, do esteemable things," is a phrase you will hear in AA. In my case, it played a major role in reducing my guilt over time. One reaches a point, though, when it is time to step aside and let people who are newer in the program benefit from these service tasks – unless there is a real void that needs to be filled, in which case one should always be looking out for someone newer in the program to groom for the role.

Carrying the Message to Other Alcoholics

Work with other alcoholics is effective in two ways. It keeps you from drinking and you can help the alcoholic prospect when no one else can.

Assuming the prospect has been passed on from the telephone service, modern AA advises twelfth steppers to visit them at home if possible. Better they see you and hear your experiences. Go in twos, men for men and women for women or a man and a woman going together is a reasonable alternative. Twelfth-steppers should work in pairs for their own protection in case they are attacked physically or a story fabricated about their behavior. Speak of alcoholism as an illness – a fatal malady – but never advise about medication.

If a member needs to go beyond the telephone service to find drinkers who want to recover, back to the old-fashioned roots of AA, the sources include doctors, hospitals and ministers of all religions. It should be productive to co-operate with other AA members through Intergroups and the like in introducing AA to these professionals so that embarrassing double approaches can be avoided. There are many AA leaflets about working with outside agencies that members should find helpful in their contacts with experts of this sort. But you may wish to check that any pamphlets you intend passing on to professionals or prospects don't contain too much god-stuff that could put people off.

First gather information on the alcoholic's background, behavior, seriousness of their condition, their problems and religious leanings. This is to see how you would like to be approached in their position.

Secondly, the approach: this will be via the family at home or in an institution via a doctor. Approach through a doctor or an institution is the preferred option. Some family doctors and most treatment centers these days will give a drug like Diazepam, formerly known as Valium, for the first four days only. This is a substitute for the tapering off by giving whisky in the earliest days. It shouldn't be taken except as a short term measure because it is another addictive drug over the long run. It will be best to wait until this part of the treatment has finished.

Always see your prospect alone if possible. I have had equally unproductive encounters when someone else was present, whether it was a prospect's spouse or a carer. On one hand, a spouse can be obstructive and wield great control over a prospect – an instance of this was where a wife wanted to stop drinking but a holiday was imminent and she mentioned that holidays were when her drinking was at its worst. We outlined some options such as checking ahead for meetings or her not going on the holiday and the husband immediately proclaimed that she had been exaggerating and the problem was not as bad as we imagined. I never saw her again. On the other hand I once went on a twelfth step call to a blind man. He sat in an armchair in the middle of the room surrounded by empty vodka bottles littering the carpet. He obviously doted on the attentions of his sympathetic lady carer who was present and decided she was a more convenient prospect than AA meetings. "I don't know why I called, I don't have a drink problem," he announced.

I usually begin by asking the drinker if they have difficulty stopping once they have started. Normally I get a good idea whether the prospect is a true alcoholic from the answer to my first question. So far I've only come across one person that wasn't. But each AA will develop a twelfth step method. A good slogan for the prospect is: "You've got to do it yourself, but you don't have to do it alone." Talk of things they won't understand at first, like the steps, can come in due time. The important points are that they don't drink, attend meetings and don't isolate. That is, they should contact AAs between meetings. "Don't raise issues of religion or non-religion," is the advice in the Big Book. "Take the line that they probably know more about it than you do. But if prospects ask why their own convictions and practices have not worked, suggest they cannot have been applied correctly."

If a prospect is not interested in your solution you may have to drop them until they change their mind. This they may do after they get hurt some more. It may actually take more courage not to pursue a lead for a while than to keep going after one. In the long run, not pushing too much may be more productive.

Once a prospect has embarked on the program by attending meetings, recommend they talk to several members they trust. Let them know you are available as a temporary sponsor if they wish, but that they may prefer to wait until they find a permanent sponsor or consult someone else. Switching between sponsers is no problem and having more than one sponsor can be a good idea.

If you are sponsoring someone who has experienced a low rock bottom they may be broke and homeless. You might give them a little financial assistance, help them look for a job or put them up for a few days. But the AA advice is not to deprive your family or creditors of money they should have and to be certain the sponsee will be welcomed by your family: "permit an alcoholic to impose on you ... and you may be destroying them rather than helping them recover.

"Those who cry for money and shelter before conquering alcohol are on the wrong track. Yet we provide these things when there is good reason. It is not the matter of giving that is in question, but when and how to give. That often makes the difference between failure and success." And if an alcoholic does not respond, there is no reason why you should neglect their family. Tell them about Al Anon.

A member of my acquaintance stresses the importance of not burdening the prospect with too much to take in at first. Again, he says the message should be: "Don't drink, go to meetings and don't isolate between meetings" – phone other members. He also points out there may be members who entered a long time ago who may be going through a rough patch and need encouragement. His advice on helping newcomers financially – from experience – is: "carry the message, not the drunk." And don't expect to get repaid.

Practice these Principles

There is a third part to step 12 that often goes unnoticed: to practice these principles in all our affairs. This means we should apply the ideas in the 12 steps across our whole lives. Not just when we are involved in helping AAs. We should behave well at home, at work and every waking hour wherever we are. We should extend the principle of helping others to our life outside AA for the program is a bridge to normal living. As a great agnostic once said: "To help each other ... is the answer to the question 'why are we here?' "

This was Albert Einstein, who did not believe in a *personal* god, but was irritated when branded an atheist. It is not true, as I've heard some religious people claim, that he "believed in God." Common sense would indicate that he's right about personal gods. There would be too many of them. They would create chaos in the universe. Yet they are what imaginary greater powers are substitutes for.

Recap of atheists 12 steps

Again, steps 1, 4, 8, 9, 10 and 12 remain the same as the original AA Twelve Steps. These can be found at the beginning of Chapter 5 *How it Works* in the Big Book.

The two adapted from the Agnostics are step 5 which I have adopted wholesale, though slightly reordered, and their step 11 which I have adopted word for word except for retaining the two words "prayer and" from the original AA Step.

The Agnostic version of Step 5 removes the greater power from AA's short list of people and things to whom and to which we will admit our bad character traits. This just seems so sensible. Trees and buses are examples of tangible greater powers members choose. It would seem odd to me if members were supposed to admit their faults to these objects. After all, step 2 talks of returning to sanity. Talking to trees and buses would seem like a step back in the wrong direction.

Even god-based alcoholics may not mind the removal of a greater power from Step Five as the third entity to which they should admit their defects. If they admit them to themselves and to another human being then surely their God will overhear the admission, too?

As for retaining prayer in step 11, I find much less trouble with the idea of prayer than the Agnostics because I simply think of it as wishing people well – purely a matter of keeping the motives in one's mind in a healthy state.

For me a prayer is just like wishing someone a safe journey. What harm can there be in spreading a little happiness and reassurance by letting someone know you wish them well. Even if you keep it to yourself, it will act as a check that one's motives are proper, which can only be improving one's own state of mind.

In the case of the other four steps I have invented new ones for atheists. I prefer my step 2 to the Agnostic version because it specifies the AA program as the route forward whereas the Agnostic version is less specific. I wish to **stick as closely as possible to the original** AA program when our experience is that it has worked well.

I prefer my step 3 for atheists over the Agnostic version because mine offers more scope to adopt any greater powers which could include the one proposed by the Agnostics: "the collective wisdom and resources of those who have searched before us."

	Atheist 12 steps
1	We admitted we were powerless over alcohol – that our lives had become unmanageable;
2 Ath	Came to believe **we couldn't solve the problem on our own, but that the group power of AA and the rest of this program** could restore us to sanity;
3 Ath	**We each nominated greater powers to remind us there are things bigger than ourselves and not to play god – then we began to let go of self-will;**
4	Made a searching and fearless moral inventory of ourselves;
5 Ag	*Admitted without reservation to ourselves and another human being the exact nature of our wrongs;*
6 Ath	**Every few months made a shortlist of our defects most in need of attention;**
7 Ath	**Made it a project to minimize one or more of our worse faults and improve our behavior;**
8	Made a list of all persons we had harmed, and became willing to make amends to them all;
9	Made direct amends to such people wherever possible, except when to do so would injure them or others;
10	Continued to take personal inventory and when we were wrong promptly admitted it;
11 AA/ Ag	Sought through prayer and meditation to improve our *spiritual awareness and understanding of the AA way of life and to discover the power to carry out that way of life;*
12	Having had a spiritual awakening as the result of these steps, we tried to carry this message to alcoholics, and to practice these principles in all our affairs.

AA original, **Bold = atheist,** *italics = based on Agnostic*

My step 3 will not only allow the adoption of the Agnostic Step 3 if a member so wishes, but also any other greater power or powers they care to adopt. It is important to look for **something new with plenty of choice** when our experience is that an aspect of the program has turned many people away from it. So this version of the step is designed to present new options and expand the membership, reaching out to those who would have been put off before.

Finally, as I say in Chapter five, my main argument for changing Steps 6 & 7 applies equally to the AA original and the version of these Steps for Agnostics. Both versions seem based on the implication that one's defects, or shortcomings, can be let go or eliminated. This simply doesn't happen in my experience and in the experience of all the people I have met and discussed this with, over more than 14 years in AA, bar a single person – whose testimony I don't accept. Therefore the object of my version of these steps for atheists – or anyone who cares to adopt them – is to identify and minimize one's character faults and keep minimizing them over time so that they become smaller and smaller and – just as one tries to achieve with one's ego – so they don't grow back.

There will be some readers who are tempted to compare these sets of steps and argue that an Agnostic one is more appropriate to Atheists and vice versa, but I'd plead against this. "AA is not a debating society," is the way many an oldtimer would put it. It is there for people to get sober. Nor have I written this book to promote debate, but purely to widen the net. As it says in AA's preamble, our primary purpose is to stay sober and help other alcoholics to achieve sobriety. This book is part of my step 12 – carrying this message to other alcoholics.

Looking beyond the various sets of 12 steps which exist, I recently heard a share in a meeting in Florida which struck a chord. The member propounded a four-stage philosophical journey for anyone in need of a program: first they come in, beaten and wooly-minded, and ask for help. They need to be welcomed and, in the case of an alcoholic, to stop drinking. Secondly they need to embrace the code on offer, say the 12 steps or the 10 commandments. Thirdly they need to question these instructions, to test if they are right for them. Fourthly they need to fashion their own beliefs. The trouble is that organizations like AA and churches don't encourage the questioning stage so people get stuck in a rut – to the detriment of their personal development and finding what is right individually for them. A proper program evolves to the point when members write steps of their own.

Chapter seven
Why Atheists need a Guide to AA

The original *Alcoholics Anonymous* was published in 1939, written by a devout Christian who used the example of a Christian god as his greater power throughout the book. However, I am an atheist alcoholic who believes many people who could be saved from drink by the AA method fail to embrace it because the god example puts them off. The reason for this book is to expand the potential numbers who might be helped. This will include those who adopt a program earlier than they would have done. It gives me a lift when I see young people getting the program. I think they've saved themselves and others around them from potential huge extra harm.

There are four points I wish to make to explain why atheists need a guide to AA: why the AA Big Book is not sufficient for them; yet the importance that they stay under the AA umbrella. First, defining one's own greater power is central to the original AA program. Even if it is on the basis of: "I don't know what it is, but I know it is." I don't follow the pattern of the original *Alcoholics Anonymous* author and use my own example throughout this book, but I will describe one of mine here. It is the group therapy of AA. This greater power is the AA program's meetings, members and literature. One of the most powerful reasons that AA meetings work is because members understand each other whereas they are not fully understood in the wider world –

even by treatment clinic professionals if they are not addicts in recovery themselves.

But atheists use their greater powers only to help in letting go of self-will in step 3 by comparing themselves with something bigger. Religious believers' higher powers are gods which direct their lives according to the Big Book. It says of a members' higher power at one stage that you now have a new employer. There is nothing of that sort of relationship for atheist AAs, yet they still need to find inspiration to lead a better life and help others. They will find no such inspiration in a book which they believe is god-based. Some religious-based members' god and higher power may be one and the same. But where these readers choose a greater power in addition to their god, they will effectively have two gods since the greater power of the original program is a duplicate or substitute god. Whereas atheists have none. That is why we have to approach the steps differently and where this book is offered as a solution.

The Big Book says AA members need more than a mere code of morals or a better philosophy of life. "If that was sufficient to overcome alcoholism, many of us would have recovered long ago. But the needed power wasn't there. We had to find a power by which we could live, and it had to be our own conception of a power greater than ourselves." It said the Big Book's main object was to enable members to find their greater powers. (Chapter 5: Step Three.)

I think the equivalent central theme of this book is to derive inspiration from our non-religious ideas of spirituality. This is the equivalent path for atheists wishing to improve their behavior and help others.

From this it follows that atheists are operating without a safety net. They have no god to do some of the work for them, though they have the support of fellow members. Therefore I believe they need to make sure they apply themselves to their program (the serious and sincere meaning of spirituality) and to disregard the idea that the steps are merely suggestions – don't believe that you can take it or leave it.

There are certain ideas we pitch to prospects to get them through the door. The idea that the steps are merely suggested is one of those. No member I've met likes to be told what to do. But in my view it is worth doing the steps thoroughly to become a happy, contented, non-drinking alcoholic rather than stopping drinking and just coming to meetings which is a halfway house.

The anonymity issue is another feature of AA that helps get prospects through the door. We preserve each other's anonymity, so it is up to the individual member whether they let their anonymity go over time. Most of us do. I have reached the point where I only keep my AA membership from acquaintances connected with getting work. Though I happily tell them I don't drink. But anonymity was an important protection for me at first.

In a similar vein, with the program being a journey, we encourage members to be selfish in the early stages to get through the withdrawals, but later we hope to be unselfish, thinking more of others and how we can contribute to humanity. It is only by getting through the door in the first place and getting through the withdrawals that we eventually become happy, well behaved, useful members of society.

So it is acceptable to tell newcomers a slightly different story to get them through the door, than the one we need to get us to rewarding places on the later journey. It is acceptable to say at first that these steps are suggested, but later to explain that this is in the same way it is suggested that you wear a parachute when you step out of an airplane.

I once sponsored Frank who sometimes came to meetings, sometimes drank. When he shared he'd say I haven't done this, I haven't read that, and then he'd say: "but that's good enough for me, today." I stopped sponsoring him and someone else tried, but also to no avail. When I went to his funeral after he'd died of drink I thought it wasn't really good enough, was it Frank?

In any event, this is the first reason atheists need an additional text to *Alcoholics Anonymous:* because they have to rely on a non-religious spiritual strength to pull them through whereas the Big Book suggests a greater power and/or god.

Secondly there is a Chapter *to agnostics* in the original AA book as well as a quotation from Herbert Spencer about openmindedness: "There is a principle which is a bar against all information, which is proof against all arguments and which cannot fail to keep a person in everlasting ignorance – that principle is contempt prior to investigation."

So I wish to explain that while I have changed during my time in AA into an atheist from an agnostic, it is based on thorough investigation. One of my reasons for immeasurable gratitude to AA is that it led me on to this path. Partly the change to atheism stems from my reading of *The God Delusion* by Richard Dawkins in which he points out that organized religions can be positively harmful. Think of all the wars around the world based on religion from the crusades onwards right through to Islamists destroying the twin towers in New York. Jews are fighting arabs, and Indian hindus are squaring up to Pakistani moslems.

In the southern states of the US there are Christians who are history-deniers teaching their children lies about evolution and the age of the earth. More despicable child abuse on a grand scale in the present day I can't imagine. So my view of these religions is based on contempt *following* investigation. I cannot see how any god would allow these practices to be carried out in its name. However, let me just mark out Buddhism as an exception here since it is not a belief system but a process of individual development.

I can't argue about a potential creator but, as I interpret the evidence, if a creator ever existed it must have died or moved a long way away to the other side of the universe and no longer has any connection to the earth. The probabilities that there might be a god are very heavily weighted against;

Please let me reiterate that I do not have anything against any individual human being until it can be proved they have committed crimes against humanity. If you tell me you are a Christian, Jew, Moslem, whatever, I will treat you with the utmost respect and be very interested in how you interpret the AA program and how you define your greater power.

But this *we agnostics* Chapter in the Big Book is a thinly veiled advertisement for god which says: don't worry if you're not yet sure there's a god – one day you will get the message – and then there is a fairly feeble attempt at conversion. So there is no consideration in the Big Book that there might not be a god, and a substitute god in the form of a higher power is the only alternative that is offered. There is no secret that the hope is this greater power will one day turn into a god for the individual member concerned.

Once again the Big Book does not embrace atheists, and only sees agnostics as potential religious converts. Therefore a different text is needed for people who have no god and agnostics who lean more to atheism than belief in god or, in any event, who happily wish to remain an agnostic until the end of their days.

Thirdly, when I say I'm an atheist people come up to me and say how awful it is that god remains in the text of the Big Book to such an extent. AA claims to be a non-religious program, but how can this be true, they say? I will demonstrate. To see how religion was taken out of the AA program we only need to appreciate how religious it was at first, when meetings started in Akron, Ohio in 1935, and compare this with the six steps as set out in Bill W's biography – after the break with the religious-based Oxford movement – before he converted them into the twelve steps in the Big Book. I see some evidence that at this stage some religion was put back into AA. But when AAs say to me that AA is riddled with religion and is still really a religious organization, I don't think they realize how much it changed between 1935 and 1939.

So here is my paraphrasing of a description of the earliest days of AA in the Big Book *A Vision for You* Chapter 11. This following description shows the heavy reliance on a religious outlook at the start. By seeing how heavily imbued with religion their early ideas were, we can appreciate the about-turn in the opposite direction.

Bill W said that each recovery from alcoholism was a miracle. He described how he and Dr Bob met and discovered that by helping each other and trying to help other alcoholics, at first unsuccessfully, they had stayed sober themselves.

Dr Bob had admitted his alcoholism to himself, and even decided that a spiritual experience was necessary to beat it, but refused to confide it to remaining clients for fear of completely losing his livelihood and bringing more suffering to his family. After meeting Bill W he went on a final bender: but in his moment of clarity he had the idea that God would give him mastery over his problems if he faced up to them.

He spent a day risking financial ruin by making the rounds of people he had hurt and was received surprisingly well. When this was recounted in the Big Book four years later, Dr Bob had not taken a drink since.

At first, the method they used to help other alcoholics was to put them in a private room at the local hospital and taper them off booze over a few days. Then they would impress on their prospect the damage being done to his body, describe their own former inability to stop drinking after taking the first one and suggest that a spiritual experience was required to beat the disease. The third member of AA was a lawyer who beat drinking, as Bill W described it, by giving his life to the care and direction of his creator. Bill W said that in finding God he had found himself and later became a power in the church.

The fourth member was a young man who had shocked his parents by refusing to have anything to do with the church until talked into recanting by the three earliest members of AA. Bill W then returned to New York and 18 months later the remaining Akron three had recruited another seven. They had casual get-togethers most nights and one night a week had a meeting for anyone interested in a spiritual way of life. The Big Book says that when they failed with a prospect they tried to bring the person's family into a spiritual way of living.

An outside couple made their home available for meetings and many wives of alcoholics visited it to find understanding among other women familiar with their problem. They were told how, when they next stumbled, their husbands might be hospitalized and approached. Bill W described it as a haven where strangers made new friends and saw miracles. "They had visioned the Great Reality – their loving and All Powerful Creator."

No alcoholic had sunk too low to be welcomed. When justified, they were lent money and jobs were found for them. They were "wrecked in the same vessel and restored *under one God.*" (There was no room here for individual greater powers.)

Bill W said that in a hospital for the treatment of alcoholic and drug addiction in an eastern US city many AAs had felt, for the first time, the Presence and Power of God. A doctor helped by selecting suitable cases for the AA program, patients who were willing and able to recover on a spiritual basis. (It sounds as though at that stage any atheist was being cast aside as an unsuitable case for treatment.)

"God will constantly disclose more," said Bill, "but you cannot transmit something you haven't got. See to it that your relationship with Him is right and great events will come to pass for you and countless others. This is the great fact for us. Abandon yourself to God as you understand God."

Bill also said that God would show alcoholics how to create the fellowship they craved. Luckily for atheists there has been a strong chain connecting modern AAs back to the pioneers – so contact with God is not necessary. Alternative sources of information are the AA offices in various countries around the world. Communication is easy via the internet, the telephone and postal services.

Another account of the earliest AA process was written by Frank Amos – later to become a non-alcoholic trustee of AA but at the time an executive in John D Rockefeller Jnr's organization who Rockefeller sent to report on AA after he had been approached for a donation. This underlines my point about religion being stronger in the program in the earliest days. This is from page 131 of Dr Bob's biography, * *Dr Bob*:

1) An alcoholic must realize that he is an alcoholic incurable from a medical viewpoint, and that he must never again drink anything with alcohol in it;

2) He must surrender himself absolutely to god, realizing that in himself there is no hope;

3) Not only must he want to stop drinking permanently, he must remove from his life sins such as adultery and others which frequently accompany alcoholism. Unless he will do this absolutely, Dr Bob and his colleagues refuse to work with him;

4) He must have devotions every morning – a quiet time of prayer and some reading from the bible and other religious literature. Unless this is faithfully followed there is grave danger of backsliding;

5) He must be willing to help other alcoholics get straightened out. This throws up a protective barrier and strengthens his own willpower and convictions;

6) It is important, but not vital that he meet frequently with other reformed alcoholics and form both a social and a religious comradeship;

7) Important , but not vital that he attend some religious service at least weekly.

By the time Bill W came to write the twelve steps in 1939 religion had virtually been taken out of the intermediate six steps with only one reference to "whatever god we thought there was" in the sixth. These six steps were quite different from the account by Frank Amos. Almost immediately *surrender to god* had instead become *surrender to alcohol* in the first step. In the modern day I have heard people use the boxing analogy I mentioned in chapter three: you don't get in the ring with Mike Tyson – you throw in the towel. That is how you beat alcohol – by not fighting it, not attempting to control it but giving it up.

Here are the intermediate six steps from page 197 of Bill W's biography, * *Pass It On*. It may easily be seen that most of the religious slant had been extracted:

1) We admitted that we were licked, that we were powerless over alcohol;
2) We made a moral inventory of our defects or sins;
3) We confessed or shared our shortcomings with another person in confidence;
4) We made restitution to all those we had harmed by our drinking;
5) We tried to help other alcoholics with no thought of reward in money or prestige;
6) We prayed to whatever god we thought there was for power to practice these precepts.

(* The permission from AA World Services to reprint the two extracts above, and an accompanying disclaimer, is shown at the end of this chapter and in Appendix one.)

These intermediate six steps boil down to: admitted we had an alcohol problem so had to stop drinking; took stock; confessed sins; made amends; helped others; and prayed.

It seems the order was not always exactly the same at this intermediate stage – not that this has much relevance to the outcome. But here is an extract from the story of one of the first hundred AAs, *He Sold Himself Short*.

'It was different from the meetings now held. The big AA book had not been written, and there was no literature except various religious pamphlets. The program was carried on entirely by word of mouth.

The meeting lasted an hour and closed with the lord's prayer. After it was closed, we all retired to the kitchen and had coffee and doughnuts and more discussion until the small hours.

I was terribly impressed by this meeting and the quality of happiness these men displayed, despite their lack of material means. In this small group, during the Depression, there was no one who was not hard up.

I stayed in Akron two or three weeks on my initial trip trying to absorb as much of the program and philosophy as possible. I spent a great deal of time with Dr Bob, whenever he had the time to spare, and in the homes of two or three other people, trying to see how the family lived the program. Every evening we would meet at the home of one of the members and have coffee and doughnuts and spend a social evening.

The day before I was due to go back to Chicago – it was Dr Bob's afternoon off – he had me to the office and we spent three or four hours formally going through the Six Step program as it was at that time. The six steps were:

1) Complete deflation
2) Dependence on and guidance from a higher power
3) Moral inventory
4) Confession
5) Restitution
6) Continued work with other alcoholics

Dr Bob led me through all of these steps. At the moral inventory, he brought up several of my bad personality traits or character defects such as selfishness, conceit, jealousy, carelessness, intolerance, ill-temper, sarcasm and resentments. We went over these at great length, and then he finally asked me if I wanted these defects of character removed. When I said yes, we both knelt at his desk and prayed, each of us asking to have these defects taken away.'

Here is the clue that underlies my belief that the religion put back into the Twelve Steps derived from the influence of the author's firm friend and mentor, Dr Bob. Bill W's Steps Six and Seven in the original AA Twelve Steps are strongly resonant of the story above about readiness for defects to be removed and asking God to remove them. Apart from the praying to god in Dr Bob's practice of these steps, there is a clear reference to a "higher power" in his second step which I take to be a religious god.

So there is clear evidence for me that the early AAs were on the right track when they were extracting religion from the first version of the program. It is unfortunate that the pendulum swung the other way when Bill W finalized the original Twelve Steps. But it never became as religious as it had been in the first place, though I believe there are meetings where the Lord's Prayer has been introduced in the modern day.

My argument is that the Big Book, though it makes laudable attempts to be all-embracing, misses out the atheist entirely and does not make a very good job of addressing the agnostic. Therefore this companion, explanatory, supporting – call it what you will – text is required.

Here is my shorthand version of the resultant atheist 12 steps listed at the beginning of my chapter four and at the end of my chapter six: admitted we had an alcohol problem so stopped drinking; realized we couldn't do it on our own – needed AA; needed to let go of self-will; took stock; confessed sins; started a project every few months to work on one or more of our worse faults; listed people we had harmed; made amends; took stock every day; improved our spiritual awareness; helped others.

Fourthly and finally, it is important for atheist AAs to stay under the umbrella of the Alcoholics Anonymous organization for many reasons. I shall list some here under

a) Atheists need AA, b) AA needs atheists, and c) We need each other.

Atheists need AA

There is the spiritual importance of belonging to a group – and the bigger the group the better, especially if it is your greater power. As atheists, virtually the only thing that is important about greater powers is that they are big, and AA is bigger with us in it.

If atheists set up their own organization outside AA presumably they would have all the growing pains that would be avoided by staying inside a mature organization. (AA could probably do without the diversion of resources and unwanted publicity that a split would inevitably generate, even if the publicity was unwanted by both parties.)

AA is as efficient an organization run by amateurs as you are going to get.

AA needs atheists

The more of us helping each other, the more power there is to each individual to accomplish their program.

The bigger AA is the more authoritative it appears as a solution for alcoholism. This should attract more alcoholics to us, for in truth we attract very few and are successful with even fewer, even if we are the cheapest and best on the market. Widening the net is very important. Also institutions, which are often keen to use AA as a maintenance program and send their customers to us after they have dried them out, may think of us more often, the bigger and more all-embracing we appear.

Doubts about AA's claims not to be religious are held not only inside AA, but they are held externally, too. Truly embracing atheists is the best way I can think of to dispel these notions. (Why not adopt this book as approved AA literature? The author would be prepared to co-operate.)

We need each other

We understand each other as alcoholics. It doesn't matter what kind of alcoholics we are – atheists, agnostics, god-fearing – we all need each other to have an understanding audience for our shares and to help each other with the common problem of alcoholism.

However there are some differences on the spiritual side between religious believers and non-believers that are best out in the open so that we don't misunderstand each other. Religious believers are fully served by the Big Book whereas non-believers aren't. That is where this book comes in, to help those who aren't religious, and aren't sure, in the AA program – and for those who are god-based to read to understand us better if they so desire.

Further, it is felt by some that the religiousness of AA is specifically Christian. More and more potential members, especially in non-Christian areas of the world, don't feel strong identification with the Christian aspect of the original program. Many people who are not happy with the old text may find that this completely non-religious book makes it possible for them to do the program anyway. It is a complementary portal into AA.

I think the Big Book made a brave attempt, sincere in its day, to include everyone in its remit. This book may allow that dream finally to become a reality.

AAWS permission and disclaimer

Chapter eight – Recovery of the Family
To: the recovering alcoholic and the family alike

My wife said she wanted me to do something about my drinking, or she would rather I didn't come back to the house. Via my doctor and a phsychiatrist I ended up as a day patient at a clinic on the addictions course, a condition of which was attendance of AA meetings. It wasn't quite as simple as that. The psychiatrist prescribed anti-depressants but the side-effects were so bad when they kicked in after two weeks they would have affected my ability to work. I threw them away and asked to go on the addictions course instead. I later told him I was grateful to him, that I saw him as the man on the turnstile at a football match who let me into the game. I don't think he liked my compliment – he saw himself as a cut above a gatekeeper.

Luckily the course was run by a member of AA. Partly it was lucky because working professionally with alcoholics and being an AA member is not always an easy combination. She gave up the work about two years later so I was lucky to gain the benefit of her professional help. There was no pulling any wool over her eyes. It was also lucky because of the extra understanding she had, over the staff who were not recovered addicts, and of my alcoholic problem in particular.

I couldn't afford to be an in-patient so came to the arrangement to attend the clinic every Thursday for six weeks. It was a good course of lectures and meetings which included weekly aftercare. Mine was feelings meetings and there were also family meetings which my parents and two brothers attended once, but my wife gave regular attendance. My son attended for a few meetings. My parents paid my bills, I think out of a feeling that they bore some responsibility for not spotting my problem when I was a teenager.

My wife's panic attacks stopped and she gave full support from the start. Everyone close seemed to forgive me my past misdeeds early on, except my son. This was perfectly understandable as I had mistreated him on occasion up to that point. One of the things I was told if you get a craving is to remember your last, worst drunk. I had rapped him on the head as a punishment a couple of weeks before I stopped drinking – when he was aged 13 – and a lump came up on his head. I should have sent him to his room and I never hit him again. He was good at sports and said he didn't want me watching him because it put him off. I used to creep around behind bushes and poke my head around the side of the pavilion to get a look. I said to him a few years on that he had spoiled my fatherhood. He said: "well, then we're even because you spoiled my childhood." We're OK now.

This chapter summarises AA's tips for the alcoholic and the family together once the alcoholic is no longer drinking and has begun to recover. Cessation of drinking, says the Big Book, is the first step away from a highly strained, abnormal condition. A doctor said: "years of living with an alcoholic is almost sure to make any partner or child neurotic. The entire family is, to some extent, ill." Many alcoholics run to extremes such as turning into workaholics or being so enthralled by their new life that they think and talk of little else. This is a time when Al Anon, family groups at treatment centers and the like can be very helpful to the former drinker's family. After all, the alcoholic has AA meetings to attend. Why shouldn't the family have their meetings, too?

Alcoholics have to stick to a spiritual program whether the rest of the family joins them or not. The rest of the family should try Al Anon meetings, or the like, and new activities to parallel the new interests of the alcoholic if they have become moribund in the home as part of the alcoholic's sickness.

Each individual in the family should adopt a spirit of love, tolerance and understanding. In family talks there should hopefully be no heated argument, no self-pity, no self-justification and no resentful criticism. Little by little the rest of the family will see they ask too much and the alcoholic will see he/she gives too little.

They should be prepared to tell most of the family's alcoholic horror stories to newer families in the same situation and relate how the family was helped in its recovery. They should stick to their own stories, not those about third parties. But the whole truth is not necessary where past misdeeds such as sexual infidelities raise tension between partners. There is absolutely no harm in giving the impression that we are not a glum lot.

Like recovery from alcoholism, the recovery of the family is a process, not an event, in which ego deflation plays its part. The more one member of the family demands others concede, the more resentful the others will become. Borrowing from President Kennedy: ask not what other members of the family can do for you. Rather, ask what you can do for the family.

The other parent will have to come to terms with the alcoholic wanting to reclaim a greater role in running the household. Both will have become used to the non-alcoholic parent wearing the trousers. They should not be surprised at temporary impotency of male alcoholics who come off the drink but, if it persists for long, he should see a doctor.

A piece of advice I had from AA members, rather than the literature, was that children use parents as templates for their own behavior, even subconsciously, and for the life partners they choose. Therefore I warned my son and daughter that they were in danger of choosing people as partners who were not the best choice. "Don't choose a shit like I was – you deserve better," was the way I put it. It was a bit like my parenting method: "don't do what I do." I can't believe they turned out so well. It must have been the influence of the mothers. But I have done what I can in that direction since embracing the goal of sobriety.

The Big Book warns that the alcoholic may find it hard to re-establish friendly relations with the children. They may hate the alcoholic for what he/she has done to them and to the other parent. This may hang on long after the other parent has accepted the alcoholic's new way of living and thinking. In time they will see that he/she is a new person and in their own way they will show it. They may take more part in family activities. From that point on progress will be rapid.

Chapter nine – To Partners, Relatives and Friends
of the alcoholic who still drinks

A passing comment on *willpower* to introduce this chapter: most medical opinion now realizes that addicts are incapable of curing themselves by willpower. Professionals no longer say "pull yourself together" to an addict. The best way I heard it explained was that one might just as well try to cure diarrhea by willpower.

For an alcoholic's partner the help of an organization like Al Anon can be lifesaving. It teaches that alcoholism is an illness that needs treatment. If the alcoholic is still drinking it teaches non-enabling behavior. Don't buy drinks for the practicing alcoholic; don't clear away their bottles for them; do not help them to drink in any way; do not help them to solve resultant problems; make them face the consequences of their actions.

If you still love your partner but can no longer put up with the fallout from the drinking – say: "I'd rather you didn't come back to this house until you've done something about your drinking." This indicates that the parting can be temporary. You could point out the AA number in the phonebook, but you can't make the final call which will trigger AA into action. The AA member on the receiving end will need to talk to the alcoholic him or herself.

I have heard from many partners, friends and family of alcoholics that belonging to Al Anon helps them lead a more spiritual life which will not take away the alcoholic's behavior, but make life more liveable – while still living with a practicing alcoholic. But the aim is to allow the alcoholic to self-diagnose that he/she has the condition even through the fog of a befuddled drinker's mind. Many recovered alcoholics say it was the beginning of the end of their drinking when their partner joined Al Anon.

If the alcoholic attends a clinic, these often have family groups that fulfill a similar function to Al Anon. From a recovered alcoholic's perspective, it's amazing how much pain and torment loved ones will put up with for how long – and how much they'll forgive when it is over.

The wives of early AAs said they had worried what friends and relatives were thinking and saying about the situation at home, but didn't talk about it with anyone, even their own parents. They did not know what to tell the children. They became reclusive. When their partners were out drinking they feared what might come through the door later on and wished the telephone had not been invented. Alcoholics cause untold chaos and uncertainty among those closest to them.

But the wives said that most of their embarrassment proved unnecessary. They found they could let friends know the nature of their partner's illness while not needing to embarrass or harm the partner by discussing it at length. The best course with any children was not to intervene but try to promote understanding all round.

They said that after they had explained to family and friends that their partners were sick, there was a new atmosphere of sympathetic understanding.

They had often covered up to employers, reporting that their partner had some other kind of sickness when it was drink-related. The wives' advice was to let the partner do the explaining. They suggested discussing it with the partner when he was sober and in good spirits, asking what they should do if he placed them in such a position again, but being careful not to be resentful about the last time he did so.

The wives of early AA members had often been afraid of the disgrace and hard times which would befall them and the children if their partners lost their jobs. But they advised those who followed after to regard this in a different light. Maybe it would prove a blessing. It could convince the alcoholic that it would be a good idea to stop drinking.

The rest of this chapter is in the format of advice on what might work in dealing with your partner who is one of four types of alcoholic described in chapter two. Thus, the alcoholic types are repeated here, followed by the relevant advice. Chapter 8 *to wives* in the Big Book has been rendered very old fashioned by the proliferation of same gender relationships since and the fact that often the alcoholic is female. So I have made the *advice* paragraphs alternately he and she.

One – heavy drinker

Heavy drinkers would probably be insulted if called an alcoholic and claim that their drinking does no one any harm but, sometimes, the drinker is a source of embarrassment to you, their partner. Heavy drinking will slow up the drinker mentally and physically, though they do not see it. Many heavy drinkers will change their behavior before, or as soon as, it becomes a problem.

Broadly, AA advises a soft sell because alcoholics do not like being told what to do. Under these circumstances the partner may eventually bring up the subject himself. Then an approach could be that you think he ought to know the subject better, as everyone should understand the risks of drinking too much. (This includes wet brain insanity, fatal liver damage and esophageal hemorrhage when the blood can hit the ceiling, but many a true alcoholic will discount these risks until they become more immediate – by which time it may be too late.)

AA's advice to the partner/relative/friend includes: be determined her drinking is not going to spoil your relations with your children or your friends, even if your partner becomes unbearable and you have to leave her temporarily. Exercise patience and good temper or it will only be less likely that your partner will stop or moderate.

I have often heard AA members joke that they searched the Big Book for a loophole, but couldn't find one. Well, here it is. "I'm not an alcoholic, I'm a heavy drinker." To my friends who came to a few meetings with me a few years ago, but decided they were heavy drinkers I say: now it is definitely time to think again. You are barely scraping by. The wife of one left for a week to go back to her mother for a rest. Another has run away to another country to escape his debts. These are classic signs. You don't have to wait until the elevator careens into the basement, but can identify your rock bottom at any floor and get off on the way down. It is always a pleasure to see someone who makes it to AA – or Atheist AA if you will – at a younger age than I did, to think of all the harm to themselves and other people that has been avoided.

I was asked in a school talk once: "How can you tell the difference between a heavy drinker and an alcoholic?" My answer was that many young people drink a lot, but most settle down when they get to the family forming age. It is the ones who cannot moderate at this stage – when they should be paying off a mortgage or at any rate income should be channeled towards the family, a pension and the like – who should probably be diagnosing themselves as alcoholic.

Two – alcoholic out of control

Many who admit to being heavy drinkers are really alcoholics in denial. They completely lose control when drinking. Their friends think their behavior has gone over the top and is no longer funny. The drinker admits it and protests that it won't happen again. Work may suffer. Sometimes they drink in the morning and through the day. They are remorseful after serious drinking bouts and tell their partner they want to stop but they can't stay on the wagon. When they get over a spree, they think they can drink moderately next time. If your partner/relative/friend displays some of this behavior they are in danger for these are the signs of a real alcoholic.

Advice

The same principles which apply to number one should be practiced, says AA. Its advice includes: after his next binge, ask if he would really like to get over drinking for good. Do not ask that he do it for you or anyone else. Just would he *like* to? The chances are he would. So tell him what you have found out about alcoholism, that more than two million men and women, much like him, have recovered. And show him an AA book. After that, if he is lukewarm or thinks he is not an alcoholic, avoid urging him to follow our program. The seed has been planted and, sooner or later, you are likely to find him reading the book. Wait until repeated stumbling convinces him he must act, for the more you hurry him the longer his recovery may be delayed.

Three – raging alcoholic, but you can be hopeful

Alcoholics like this were once like number two, but have gone much further. Friends have gone, they can't keep a job and their home is a tip. The round of clinics and treatment centers (they used to be called asylums) has begun. Either they pathetically hang on to the idea they'll one day drink like a gentleman or they badly want to stop. The chances of AA working in the case of a raging alcoholic are good.

Advice

You may be in luck, says AA. If this alcoholic is otherwise a normal individual, your chances are good at this stage. She is practically sure to read the book and may go for the program at once. Or, probably you will not have long to wait. Again, you should not crowd her. Let her decide for herself.

Four – far gone, yet they could get well

This alcoholic may be despondent after detoxing many times. They are a violent or insane drunk. Sometimes they drink on the way home from the hospital. Perhaps they have had delirium tremens. Yet this picture may not be as dark as it looks. Many other alcoholics were just as far gone, but they got well.

Advice

The advice includes: try to have your alcoholic read about AA. His reaction may be one of enthusiasm. If already committed to an institution, but able to convince you and the doctor that he means business, give him a chance to try our method, unless the doctor thinks his mental condition too abnormal or dangerous. Some have been so impaired by alcohol that they cannot stop. Sometimes alcoholism is complicated by other disorders. But AA asserts that such cases have often had spectacular recoveries.

You may have the reverse situation, says the Big Book. Perhaps you have a partner who is at large, but who should be committed. Presumably, after committal and the passage of time, the same advice as in the paragraph above can kick in once more.

Chapter ten – To Employers
of the alcoholic who still drinks

Addressed to employers

Please refer to Chapter 10 of the Big Book.

ı

Chapter eleven – A–Z

A Anonymity. This is an especially important concept to newcomers. No member should divulge to anyone the identity of people who attended a meeting or the personal details disclosed by members. It is up to members alone whether to divulge their own membership of AA on a case-by-case basis. Even when they no longer care about anonymity generally, most members don't tell people in their workplace. They might say they no longer drink alcohol rather than saying they belong to AA. When they first start declining alcoholic drinks and ask for a *Coke Zero*, new members often expect an inquest which doesn't arise. If someone presses you to drink they often have an alcohol problem of their own. In confirmation of this, you may have done the same when you drank. Did your family and friends have to drink more just to normalize your own consumption?

B Big Book. *Alcoholics Anonymous*

B Bill W. Wrote the Big Book and was a co-founder of AA with Dr Bob. The two of them met in 1936. Bill W had already had his last drink but was still having cravings, especially when feeling lonely, and was attempting to help other alcoholics as a way of diverting himself from drinking. He visited Dr Bob, having been given his name via a church minister as someone who was also struggling with drink and had not yet stopped. Dr Bob's last drink was on 10 June, 1936, the basis for AA's anniversary.

B   Blackout. Alcoholics in blackout can behave pretty normally, or drunkenly. Or can start apparently normal and progress to drunk. But afterwards they don't know what happened. It is a lapse of memory of events of the night before or entire days before. It does not mean passing out through drinking too much, but rather not remembering what you did.

C   Chair. The opening talk at a meeting to provide something for members to think about.

C   Change. I have changed for the better in AA. It isn't always evident to me if I look back to yesterday, but it is always apparent when I look back six months.

In a foreword to the Big Book, Dr Silkworth said the remedy for an alcoholic would have to include **"psychic change."** When you look up the word psychic there is nothing mystical about it. I take it to mean a change in mental attitude. I hope this simplifies the journey for any reader of the Doctor's Opinion which, to repeat, can be found at the front of the Big Book.

D Denial. This is simply a person's denial that they have a drink problem. Since we regard alcoholism as a self-diagnosed illness, we don't argue with anyone over the category they put themselves in. Alcoholism is the disease that tells you that you don't have it. The end of denial is part of the first step.

D Disease. Alcoholism is a disease. The United Nations says so. So you shouldn't feel guilty about having it. It's not your fault. Mind you, you've plenty of other faults. But this program helps you to reduce those over time.

D Dr Bob. See Bill W.

E Einstein. Was an agnostic genius who said the reason we are here is to help each other. Don't let religious people tell you he believed in God. It isn't true.

F Faith. There is no need for blind faith. Look around you in the meeting room and see what AA has done for others. You will find your faith in the process from the evidence before you.

F Fun. We have not been cast up on the beach to lead a miserable life.

F Functioning alcoholic. Not yet on skid row. One who believes they display the outward appearance of a normal lifestyle, but goes to amazing lengths to hide their disease.

G God. There isn't one.

H HALT. Hungry, angry, lonely, tired. These are indicators of vulnerability to a relapse. Eat, calm down, phone a friend in AA, sleep.

H Honesty. Always part of a successful program.

I I. Self is NOT what it is about except in the early stages of the program. Then you must address yourself. Later, do something for others.

J Joy. We weren't thrown up on the beach to be miserable.

K Key to the spiritual value of the steps for me: managing my expectations down to a lower level. After applying a little humility my estimation of my own importance is lower along with the outcomes I deserve. So I am always pleasantly surprised.

L Letting Go. This is the spiritual core of the program for me, Step 3, requiring trust in the outcome. Here blind faith is required on the first occasion before experience builds up a body of evidence that it works. Do your spadework well before handing over to others who will make the decisions. Do not bully or manipulate these people.

M Meetings. Keep going every week even if you don't need one. It's money in the bank, petrol in the tank for when you do need one but there isn't one nearby. Try to get to 90 meetings in 90 days at the beginning.

M Motives. Make all the difference. Examine them when determining a course of action. Be honest about them with yourself. Keep them pure. Then you will know that you are behaving well, even if someone else doubts your motives. It may help this other person to behave well, too, if they understand what your motives are. But it must not matter to you what they think of you. That would be to take their inventory, which we do not do.

N Never. You never have to drink again.

O Outcomes. Are always better than I expected due to lowering my expectations.

P Practicing alcoholic. Is an alcoholic still drinking as opposed to one who has stopped. You don't get rid of alcoholism. You just stop drinking and enjoy life.

P Prayer. Is a way of formulating thoughts and plans in your mind. To whom are you addressing your prayers, then, an atheist has asked me defiantly. The answer is that the alcoholic part of my brain is communicating with the area which contains my AA program. You can convey these as messages to ... something / someone if you wish. But if any messages come back the other way you had best call for the men in white coats. If you pretend you hear messages coming back the other way as a means of procuring an income from gullible individuals this is fraud and you should surrender yourself to the nearest law enforcement officer immediately.

P Promises. We will be amazed as these promises materialize if we work for them: new freedom, new happiness, we will not regret the past nor wish to shut the door on it, we will comprehend the word serenity and know peace, we will see how our experience can benefit others, feelings of uselessness and self-pity will disappear, we will lose interest in selfish things and gain interest in our fellows, fear of people and of economic insecurity will leave us, we will intuitively know how to handle situations which used to baffle us.

117

P Psychic change. See change

Q Question. Am I an alcoholic? See chapter two.

R Resentments. Carrying on from the Step 3 theme of self-will, the most common sign of resultant problems – and an alcoholic's spiritual sickness – are resentments. They can lead to a drink, which could be fatal. Personal relationships are their root cause says the Big Book. But Step 4 teaches us how to draw their sting.

S Sobriety. Not just teetotal but the life of a happy, contented and responsible individual, on a program, to whom others look up.

S Spiritual. Greater than the sum of the parts in the field of human interaction (deriving from the affinity one feels in a group). I am uplifted by the sense of belonging and I take the program extra seriously and sincerely in all I do. There is a much longer definition in chapter four under *Letting Go.*

S Sponsor. We need a sponsor as a personal guide to the program. Pick someone whose sobriety you admire and ask them to be your sponsor.

S Surrender. We surrender to alcohol, not God. Admit that alcohol has beaten you and throw in the towel – this is the real victory. In this boxing analogy you don't get in the ring with Mike Tyson. That is how you beat alcohol – by not fighting it, not attempting to control it but giving it up.

T Telephone. It's always OK to call. You will be doing a favor for the person you're calling as well. The only exception is when everyone in a group calls a newcomer – who could be overwhelmed.

T Types of problem drinker. See chapter two.

U Unity. Each AA member is different. Every AA meeting has its own feel. But we all stick together to help and learn from each other.

V Very simply. Don't drink and go to meetings.

W White-knuckling. This is giving up drinking by yourself – where one can stay off alcohol for a period but will remain a dry drunk – which is a miserable existence.

W Willingness. Your time will come when it is appropriate to get on with the steps. Don't prevaricate at this stage – just get on with them.

W Willpower. Most medical opinion now realizes that addicts are incapable of curing themselves by willpower. Professionals no longer say "pull yourself together" to an addict. The best way I heard it explained was that one might just as well try to cure diarrhea by willpower.

X Xperience, strength and hope. Required structure of any chair you are asked to give.

X Xtraordinary. The time when you first realize someone is in trouble – not because they're asking for help, but because they've lost control over a trivial issue. They might be shouting at you, but you can say: "What's wrong? Tell me about it."

Y You. Are the most important person in the early stages while you sort yourself out. Then it becomes others who need help the most.

Z RealiZation that you belong. This is a spiritual awakening. But there are others: Realization that you never need to drink again. Realization that you don't want a drink anymore – the craving has gone and even if it reappears you are fully equipped to deal with it. Realization that you are serious and sincere about the program.

Appendix one

AA permissions

My plan for a companion volume to *Alcoholics Anonymous* needed a rethink when I was denied permission to reprint from that book as may be gathered from the letter I received, shown below.

ALCOHOLICS ANONYMOUS WORLD SERVICES, INC.
475 RIVERSIDE DRIVE, NEW YORK, NY10115 (212) 870-3400
(Between 119th and 120th Streets)

A.A. **AAWS**	Please direct all communications to:- **GRAND CENTRAL STATION** **PO BOX 459** **NEW YORK, NY 10163** **FAX# 212-870-3003**

August 23, 2010

To:- Vince Hawkins

I apologize for the delay in responding to your request to adapt and reprint large quantity of excerpts from the Big Book, *Alcoholics Anonymous* for inclusion in your future publication entitled *Atheists Alcoholics Anonymous*.

Alcoholics Anonymous World Services, Inc. has been charged with the responsibility of preserving the integrity of the AA message, as articulated in AA literature, and of protecting and preserving AA's intellectual property rights – copyrights, trademarks and service marks, etc – which have been entrusted to AAWS for safekeeping.

Therefore the reprinting and adapting of large quantity of AA material from the Big Book, *Alcoholics Anonymous* would tend to dilute the credibility of the Big Book and would cause a likelihood of confusion in those seeking help within the AA program. Additionally, your publication would imply that AA endorses and has an affiliation with Atheists Alcoholics Anonymous.

Therefore we cannot grant you permission to reprint and adapt material from the Big Book, *Alcoholics Anonymous* or any other AA material for inclusion in your publication.

Sincerely,

From:- Darlene Smith
Intellectual Property Administrator

www.aa.org

This saved me from the easy way out because it would have been lazy simply to base my book on great swathes of the original with God taken out. Let me express my gratitude to AA for forcing me to do a proper job of work and pen a whole book.

This is just another very small piece of gratitude on top of the mountainous list which begins with being alive. So far I've had 13 years without a drink and I believe I would have lost my life to it in six months if I'd continued drinking rather than stopping on October 6, 1998. The same will apply if I take a drink in the future. One of the other items on my list of gratitude to AA is that it has facilitated my journey to atheism through the (long, drawn out in my case) process of defining a greater power or powers. It has enabled me to frame my views on gods and religion.

However this tale has another twist because I subsequently discovered that the copyright on the first and second editions of *Alcoholics Anonymous* has run out in the USA. Therefore I must make it clear that these are the editions I refer to in this work. (See the following two websites: www.silkworth.net/gsowatch/1939/uslaw.htm & www.anonpress.org/faq/files/read.asp?fID=239)

Subsequently, AA World Services has kindly granted me permission to reprint from the biographies of Dr Bob and Bill W, *Dr Bob* and *Pass It On,* (See pp100–102 above) in return for my publishing the following disclaimer: *Permission to reprint these excerpts does not mean that AAWS has reviewed or approved the contents of this publication, or that AAWS necessarily agrees with the views expressed herein. AA is a program of recovery from alcoholism only – use of these excerpts in connection with programs and activities which are patterned after AA, but which address other problems, or in any other non-AA context, does not imply otherwise. Additionally, while AA is a spiritual program, AA is not a religious program. Thus, AA is not affiliated or allied with any sect, denomination, or specific religious belief.*

The latest twist in May 2013 is that AAWS says: "if you have not included any adapted text material (other than the steps) or reprinted large segments from the Big Book, AAWS would have no objection to you selling your publication outside of the US."

So I wish to thank AA once more. Thanks also, beyond measure, to my family including my first wife who have forgiven me my past misdeeds. I must always try to remember, too, that it is better to forgive than to be forgiven. Thanks to the program, eventually this has included forgiving myself.

Appendix two

Further reading:- Richard Dawkins' *The God Delusion* and *The Greatest Show on Earth: The Evidence for Evolution*

If AA is the biggest magnet for my gratitude, another is the author of the two books mentioned above. In my search for spirituality, a higher power and to formulate my attitude to religion these works helped me immensely. It was as though Richard Dawkins gave form to my ideas on atheism through his words. He confirmed what I believed and strengthened it with authority through his proof of evolution. But the kernel of his argument against the existence of god is in *The God Delusion*, chapter 4: Why there is almost certainly no God.

Richard Dawkins begins by saying the clincher for most believers in god is thinking that humans, animals and nature couldn't have happened by chance. There must have been a creator, or designer, at work.

Well, it is true that it didn't happen by chance. But it didn't happen by design either. Instead of a creator in the biological world there was Darwin's natural selection at work. And though Darwinism may not be directly relevant to the inanimate world – cosmology for example – it raises our consciousness in areas outside its original territory of biology. Darwin teaches us to seek out graded ramps of slowly increasing complexity.

Scientifically savvy philosopher Daniel Dennett pointed out that evolution counters one of the oldest ideas we have: the idea that it takes a big fancy smart thing to make a lesser thing. You'll never see a horseshoe making a blacksmith.

Darwin's discovery of a workable process that does that very counter-intuitive thing is what makes his contribution to human thought so revolutionary, and so loaded with the power to raise consciousness.

What is it that makes natural selection succeed as a solution to the problem of improbability, where chance and design both fail at the starting gate? The answer is that natural selection is a cumulative process. Real life seeks the gentle slopes at the back of Mount Improbable, while creationists are blind to all but the daunting precipice at the front.

So there is no God around now. But was there once a creator of life that laid down the necessary DNA-like substance to get life going?

Dawkins says "no" on the grounds of statistical probability. He looks at the number of 'Goldilocks' planets in the universe with liquid water, needed for life, neither frozen into ice nor boiled away to steam – those in just the right comfortable orbit around a sun. Earth has other coincidental supporting factors such as Jupiter's gravity vacuuming up potentially harmful asteroids. It has been estimated there are between one billion and 30 billion planets in our galaxy and about 100 billion galaxies in the universe. Knocking off a few noughts for ordinary prudence, a billion billion is a conservative estimate of the number of available planets in the universe. "Now, suppose the origin of life, the spontaneous arising of something equivalent to DNA, really was a quite staggeringly improbable event. Suppose it was so improbable as to occur on only one in a billion planets. Even with such absurdly long odds, life will still have arisen on a billion planets.

So if there was no God with a hand in the creation of life ... what about the creation of the universe, or universes – the beginning of everything?

Dawkins doesn't touch on this specifically, but it isn't difficult to follow his raising of consciousness argument and project that there will be a rational explanation for what we don't understand at the moment. And there is no reason why it should include a god. That would be just one of the many alternatives we might postulate via our imagination. Statistical chances, then, are that the truth lies elsewhere. Religious people tend to say: 'don't bother looking for the truth – let us put it down to God'. But as the gaps in our knowledge keep closing and God is pushed out of these gaps, the chances of there being a god at all get slimmer and slimmer.

For me, then, the door is only open by the faintest sliver on the chance of a god with a hand in creation. I see no evidence of any influence on world affairs since. If there was one, my favourite theory because it has a certain elegance would be god as suicide bomber or incompetent chemistry schoolmaster who blew himself up in the Big Bang. But even that is a very big "if."

Appendix three

Invitation to write a page for publication in *Atheists Daily Reflections: Non-AA-approved.*

The format will comprise a page per day of the year.

1) Please select a favorite short quotation from this book and say why it is your favorite or how it has special meaning for you. Alternatively simply add a comment you think might help another alcoholic.

2) Indicate that you assign copyright to Vince Hawkins.

3) Then indicate how you would like to be identified. A suggestion would be *Paul X of Seattle.*

4) Send one entry per email to vince_hawk@hotmail.com

Send in as many entries as you wish, though we suggest not more than twelve – one for each step.

If the comment is on a Step it will be allocated to the appropriately numbered month of the year, so Step 7 under a day in July. If you wish to nominate a particular date, maybe the first day of your sobriety for example, we will do our best to accommodate you but can make no guarantee.

Then watch out for the future publication of the book, *Atheists Daily Reflections.*